The Politics of Expertise in Congress

The Politics of
Expertise
in Congress

THE RISE AND FALL OF THE OFFICE OF
TECHNOLOGY ASSESSMENT

Bruce Bimber

State University of New York Press

Published by
State University of New York Press

For information, address the State University of New York Press,
State University Plaza, Albany, NY 12246

Production by Bernadine Dawes • Marketing by Bernadette LaManna

Library of Congress Cataloging-in-Publication Data

Bimber, Bruce A. (Bruce Allen), 1961–
    The politics of expertise in Congress : the rise and fall of the
Office of Technology Assessment / Bruce Bimber.
        p.   cm.
    Includes bibliographical references and index.
    ISBN 0–7914–3059–6 (alk. paper). — ISBN 0–7914–3060–X (pbk. :
alk. paper)
        1. Technology assessment—United States. 2. United States.
Congress. Office of Technology Assessment. 3. Technology and
state—United States. I. Title.
T174.5.B56 1996
338.97307—dc20   96–7386
                                                      CIP

1 2 3 4 5 6 7 8 9 10

For Laura

CONTENTS

PREFACE

In 1820, Thomas Jefferson commented on a problem whose gravity has increased in the many decades since: the function of expert knowledge in public decisions. In correspondence with William Jarvis, the ex-President remarked that political power must never be yielded to experts on the judgment that citizens are too poorly informed to make wise decisions for themselves.[1] His observation is simple, and comes as no surprise from one of the leaders of the founding. Jefferson was reflecting on the working of the judiciary in this letter, but his point derives from a broader conviction, namely that democratic public policy must indeed stand upon a foundation of the public will, even when it also demands special expertise thought to be beyond the reach of the public.

Jefferson offered a resolution to this dilemma of uniting expert knowledge and public determination, but his solution comes up short, despite lofty optimism. The man who had, two years earlier, founded the University of Virginia explained in his letter that when the public was deemed insufficiently expert to participate in public decisions, then that public's judgment must be better educated—not set aside in favor of the knowledge of professional experts. No good democrat could disagree with Jefferson. But this advice provides scant working guidance to those interested in the details of the contemporary policy system. Problems such as regulating the telecommunications industry, controlling air pollution, choosing military weapons systems, or constructing a national health care policy demand more expertise than can be asked of even the best educated and most attentive citizenry or most specialized representatives. Clearly, experts must participate in policymaking, but how?

This book considers a modern remedy to the problem of experts' roles in democratic decisions that Jefferson could not have foreseen: the public think tank, joined institutionally to the policy process but vested with no political authority of its own. The book explores the relationship between Congress and one such organization, the Office of Technology Assessment, or OTA.

Congress voted to create OTA in 1972, during a period when some legislators were concerned with the social effects of new technology, and when nearly all were intensely interested in shoring up Congress' independence from the executive. OTA functioned for roughly two decades as a small unit of the legislative branch, employing scientists and other experts at the task of informing congressional policy-making. OTA served as an expert advisor on policy, not an official participant in decision-making or voting.

In 1995, Congress voted to terminate OTA's operations. This decision was part of what was then being called the Republican Revolution. The elimination of the agency was a product of the politics of budget cutting, calculated not so much to make a significant reduction in appropriations as to demonstrate Congress' willingness to make cuts close to home. It is a conspicuous feature of the political logic of the federal budget that OTA came to an abrupt end not because its budget had grown too large, but precisely because it was so small.

From the perspective of institutional politics, OTA's termination was consistent with other changes underway in the legislature in 1995. From the perspective of policy problems, its termination was ironic, since it came at a time when many legislators—especially the new Speaker of the House, Newt Gingrich—were experiencing a revival of interest in the social implications of new technology. Indeed, one of the themes of this study is that the politics of expertise cannot be understood only by asking questions about policy *per se*, about uncertainty, or about how one calculates the costs and benefits of alternative responses to public problems. These are intertwined with matters of institutional imperatives and political structure.

During its two decades, OTA functioned as a very modest instrument for joining the knowledge of the expert with the judgment of the public's elected representatives, and one suspects that Jefferson himself would have approved of this arrangement. During that time, OTA evolved through distinct stages. This evolution reflects a search for an operating strategy appropriate to its institutional environment. After trying and discarding two unsuccessful approaches, it devised what I call the *strategy of neutrality*. That strategy reveals how technical knowledge can be important to politics, how institutional structure can shape the production of knowledge, and, more importantly for Jefferson's concerns, it illuminates limits on the authority of that form of knowledge in healthy democratic politics.

This book was motivated by my own interest in the modern aspects of Jefferson's problem, the nature of knowledge and the problem of its place in the operation of democratic government. Having been educated once in California as an electrical engineer and then again in New England as a political scientist, I have profited immensely from systematic exposure to two strikingly different realms of knowledge and action. As an engineer, I learned about the application of positivism and the mathematical representation of physical phenomena. As a political scientist, I have been engaged in debates about what limits exist on our ability to capture social phenomena with comparable nomothetic generalizations.

Indeed, it is fascinating to observe two trends in our knowledge of knowledge over recent decades. At roughly the same time that the philosophy and sociology of science were mounting epistemological challenges to the positivism of the physical sciences, mathematically inclined social scientists were struggling to import that same positivism into analysis of social action and values. This is not a book about methodology or epistemology, but in the course of several years of observing OTA's scientists making claims about the state of the world to the most political of all audiences— Congress—I have been struck with a recurrent thought about those subjects. It is that one of the central issues at stake in OTA's relationship with Congress is also at stake in academic debates about positive social science: the separability of facts and values. The possibility of isolating objective truths from human values, and the ability to capture what is most important about public life with science, shapes both experts' attempts to inform policy-making and scholars' struggles to define methodology for understanding political action. This is an underlying theme of *The Politics of Expertise in Congress*.

With this said, I should clarify my own methodological position here. In this effort, but certainly not in all my other work, I have found deductively framed qualitative research more illuminating than inductive quantification or other tenets of positivism—in this case not so much out of a prior methodological commitment but because of the nature of the problem and the evidence available about it.

This study emerged from my doctoral dissertation at MIT, and I owe a lasting debt to the scholars there at the time who introduced me to the study of social and political phenomena: Walter Dean Burnham, Joshua Cohen, Ken Keniston, Leo Marx, Mark Peterson (at Harvard), Merritt Roe Smith, Charles Stewart III, Richard Valelly, and Charles Weiner. The research for the book took the form of approximately a hundred interviews on Capitol Hill and an exhaustive examination of documents and records in congressional committee offices, the Senate Library, the Library of Congress, and the Office of Technology Assessment. The study would have been impossible were it not for Congress' tradition of openness to scrutiny by scholars, the press, and individual citizens—a tradition which is itself a marker of sound democracy. I am much indebted to the legislators and their staff who spoke with me and expressed their views about the work of Congress. Much of the institutional capacity of Congress resides in its staff, and I am especially appreciative of their willingness to share their expertise with me. Most staff spoke with me on the condition of anonymity, and so while their words are set off in quotation marks, I do not provide specific citations. Interviews conducted on the record are cited as such.

I am grateful to the former staff of the Office of Technology Assessment. They offered me time, trust, and access to a wealth of records and archival documents. They let me into their offices while they worked, let me observe their operations, and continued to be available to me even as they went about their final tasks of closing down the agency. In particular I want to thank Roger Herdman, John Gibbons, Russell Peterson, Emilio Daddario, Eugenia Ufholz, Martha Dexter, Gail Kouril, and especially Jim Jensen, at OTA.

I also owe a debt to the staff and scholars of the Governmental Studies Program at the Brookings Institution, first for providing a year-long research fellowship and then for welcoming me back on occasion during the writing of this book. The sixth floor of 1775 Massachusetts Avenue remains one of the best places in Washington from which to learn about American democracy. In particular I want to thank Nancy Davidson, Steve Hess, Tom Mann, Bert Rockman, Susan Stewart, and Kent Weaver at Brookings.

Other colleagues around the country have taught me much, as well as made scholarship enjoyable, and I would like to single out three for special notice: David Guston, Jessica Korn, and Katie Dunn Tenpas.

My greatest debt is to my wife, Laura Mancuso, to whom I owe far more than can be expressed in a page of professional acknowledgments. She gave immeasurably during the preparation of this work, as a companion and inspiration, and I will not forget it.

Chapter 1

Knowledge and Power

Congress is awash in policy information. No institution in the United States is the focus of a greater volume of studies and analysis exploring public problems and recommending solutions. The flow of information through the office of even the most junior legislator can be overwhelming. Analysis of policy problems arrives in a river of books, papers, articles, memoranda, reports, videotapes, and electronic mail. It is presented in hearings, in private meetings, through the electronic "Net," at fund-raisers, in phone conversations, and over meals in Washington's restaurants.

Behind this flood is an enormous corps of policy experts. The experts have many designations—researcher, analyst, scientist, economist, professor, advisor, staff member. Many do not work for Congress directly, but are located in think tanks, lobbying organizations, corporations, universities, and, most importantly, in the agencies of the executive branch. The numbers of these external experts have increased dramatically in recent decades. At the end of World War II, only a handful of private policy think tanks were at work in Washington; at the end of the Cold War there were over one hundred, the largest ones spending tens of millions of dollars annually on the analysis of policy problems.[1] Several thousand advisory committees of experts have sprung up, forming what has been called the "fifth branch" of government.[2] This growth in think tanks and advisory committees has been outpaced by the explosion in interest groups, which provide studies and analyses—brains—along with their infamous brawn. The sevenfold growth in the number of groups since the mid-70s[3] has not only produced historic changes in how elections are financed and run, but has also provided new channels through which expert information about policy can reach legislators. The commissioning of studies has become a part of the price of admission to policy debates for some interest groups.[4]

An internal corps of experts also provides information to Congress, generating their own analysis as well as distilling the external flood for legislators. Committee staff, personal staff, and experts at the legislature's three analytic agencies—the Congressional Research Service, the Congressional Budget Office, the General Accounting Office—provide the backbone of Congress' information-gathering system and make it the most well-staffed legislature in the world.[5] The spectacular growth in staff is one of the most commonly cited features of the modern Congress. Even after consolidation of committees and subcommittees and staff reductions in 1995, Congress' staff was about five times larger than at the end of World War II.

THE ROLE OF EXPERTS IN CONGRESS

Perhaps the most remarkable feature of these internal and external experts for Congress is that their roles in policy-making are somewhat of an enigma. Experts clearly have the potential to shape every step in the congressional policy process. They can influence agendas by their contributions to what Kingdon calls the "policy stream," and by helping define what is a problem and what is not.[6] Experts have the potential to influence legislators' policy preferences by illuminating connections between choices and political outcomes, and they can shape public dialogue by contributing to discourse about politics. They can shape the success of policy implementation, not only by their contribution to the content of legislation, but also by their role in oversight and appropriation activities.

But to say that experts can and sometimes do shape policymaking in all these ways reveals very little about the real nature of experts' power and about their actual impact on policy outcomes. Studies of roll-call voting, elections, agenda-setting, oversight, and even staffing arrangements have failed to produce a useful portrait of the role of expertise in the congressional policy process or of the strategies and goals of experts themselves. For instance, a common claim from research on Congress is that legislators are rarely well-informed about public policy, because the system of electoral incentives to which they respond does not reward the acquisition of substantive knowledge, and instead encourages empty position-taking. Moreover, the great demands on legislators' time are believed to prevent the development of more than a superficial understanding of complex problems. Congress is traditionally described as the branch of government least capable of informing its work with policy analysis and substantive expertise.[7] Congress' comparative advantage is said to be consensus, compromise, and representation, rather than expertise, analysis, and administration.[8]

Yet this common view appears to contradict the fact that Congress has built itself such an extensive system of experts over the last two decades, expanding the size and capability of its staff, and establishing new internal agencies. Indeed, legislators themselves often advance the view that expertise is a significant force in legislative politics. Former Speaker Jim Wright has written that there is "a direct link between knowledge, power, and the Congress."[9] Russell Long, Chair of the Senate Finance Committee for fifteen years, provides a memorable example. Respected not only for his political skills, he has been called an "inspired maestro" for his extensive knowledge of the tax code.[10] During debate over the landmark Budget Reform Act of 1974, Senator Lee Metcalf, Chair of the Joint Committee on Congressional Operations, remarked in a floor statement that "information is the name of the game in budget control."[11]

One need look no further than the debate over any major piece of legislation, from the successful tax reform bill of 1986 to the failed health care reform bills of 1994, to find anecdotal corroboration of Wright's and Metcalf's claims. The influence of experts is found in the structure and content of legislation, in its timing, even in the strengths of political coalitions. Fenno's now historical portrait of committees provides the most authoritative support for these observations. Fenno found that specialization and the development of substantive expertise increase the power of individual members of Congress in their pursuit of reelection, public policy, and professional influence and status.[12]

So Congress is said to be institutionally disinterested and ill-suited to the acquisition and use of policy expertise, but it nonetheless is immersed in a tide of expertise that is visible at every step of the legislative process. Experts continue to gravitate toward a Congress often believed not to be listening. And legislators are said to find expertise not particularly useful to their political pursuits, but have nonetheless developed policy staffs and dedicated information-gathering and -analyzing agencies.

These contradictions are characteristic of the muddled state of affairs in our understanding of the politics of expertise in contemporary American government, especially in the case of Congress. While matters of expertise have always attracted the attention of a few researchers, their efforts have generally made limited headway in producing useful claims about what experts do, why they do it, and what difference it makes. This is particularly true for Congress, where the public often expects legislators to be both Burkean trustees informed by the best expert analysis, and instructed delegates responsive directly to constituent's wishes, as well or ill informed as they may be. The "limits on policy analysis," to use Lindblom's term, have been well documented in critiques of rational, deductive models of policy-making.[13] These critiques have shown the fallacy of believing that scientific techniques are adequate or sufficient for treating problems in the realms of values.

But rejecting the plausibility of linear, reductionist models of the policy process does not explain much about the role of the immense volume of analysis and information about policy that is nonetheless directed at Congress—almost as if the institution did make policy in a rational, analysis-driven fashion. Nor does it indicate much about how experts respond to their environment or what arrangements for informing policy might be most attractive normatively. Studies of "knowledge utilization" in politics have sought to provide an empirical portrait of this problem by attempting to uncover patterns in the use of expert knowledge by political actors, including members of Congress.[14] But despite a number of claims about correlations among variables for forms of knowledge use, issue salience, degree of political conflict, and so forth, these studies have left an unconvincing literature characterized by inconsistent findings and no underlying theoretical foundation.[15] Knowledge utilization studies make a case that the relationship between information use and political conditions is chaotic, complex, and non-linear, rather than simple or straightforward.

THE PROBLEM OF POLITICIZATION

This book is an exploration of one aspect of these problems concerning the politics of expertise, in the setting of the U.S. Congress.[16] Its primary subject is a problem that surfaces in virtually every discussion of expertise and politics, whatever the context, and that lies beneath the surface of many empirical and normative aspects of the politics of expertise: neutrality and politicization. Whether experts are neutral and "objective" or politicized and "biased" is a question that is never far from any conversation about expertise in politics. The traditional ideal of the policy expert is someone who brings the neutral authority of science to bear on policy. Indeed, acknowledging the distinction between expert and non-expert requires acceptance of a technical standard of knowledge in which objectivity is an important part.

Yet few serious observers of politics believe that facts and values can be separated cleanly. Scientists need not work for the Tobacco Institute for their motives to be questioned. Decades of very public battles among experts over the environment, social problems, and almost every other policy issue, have demonstrated the capacity of experts to bring political alliance and commitment to their work. It is common to ask whose experts should be believed, whether expert claims must be discounted because of the political interests of the experts themselves, and how government can best elicit advice from experts that is unshaded by partisanship or ideology.

These problems lie at the root of many issues involving the politics of expertise. This book's main purpose is to offer an explanation for one kind of variation in patterns of politicization and neutrality on the part of experts. It examines factors that shape the provision of expertise and experts' performance against the standard of political disinterestedness. Along the way, the book looks at how information is used in politics, at its place in the policy process, and at its contribution to institutional politics within Congress and between Congress and the executive. It examines questions about what legislators want from experts, and about how their demands shape what experts do.

By focusing on the subject of expert neutrality and politicization, this study examines what I believe to be the core dynamic in the politics of expertise, namely the relationships between experts and politicians. The chief premise of this study is that one cannot understand information in politics divorced from an understanding of the relationship between the experts who produce it and the policy-makers who use it. Questions about expertise are sometimes framed abstractly, in terms of inherent connections between knowledge and power. Inquiring just about Bacon's nexus between information or expertise on the one hand, and policies or political decisions on the other, as is often done, frames the problem inadequately. It is the underlying relationship between producers and users of information that is where the links between power and information are forged. Expertise is not a disinterested and detached resource to political actors; nor is its legitimacy purely a function of technical credibility. As we will see throughout this discussion, when legislators talk about expertise, they almost invariably speak in terms of its origins. They do not understand analysis, policy studies, and other forms of expert information in isolation from their understanding of the people who have produced it. Knowledge does not itself necessarily convey power; rather, power frequently lies in the relationship between producers and consumers of knowledge. Gaining a better understanding of basic questions about the politics of expertise, then, requires a close look at that relationship.

There is a prevailing view about the state of politicization of experts, and it serves as a starting point for my analysis. In the traditional view, experts tend to grow more politicized and less neutral the longer they are exposed to politics and the closer they come to the exercise of power. Not really a theory so much as an observation or article of faith, this view holds that neutrally competent, politically uncommitted experts and administrators cannot exist in a state of equilibrium with political patrons.[17] Policy-makers are believed to want experts to serve their political needs, not to provide neutral pronouncements that may hurt their political objectives as much as help them. Politicians' demands for politically supportive expertise tends to root out neutral experts and replace them with politically loyal experts; hence, a long-term trend toward the increasing politicization of experts develops. In this view, the goal of informing government with the best expert information, unshaded by partisanship, is not fully attainable in the long run.

This book argues that the prevailing view of the increasing politicization of expertise is inadequate. It is an approximation that holds under certain circumstances, and it leads to overly pessimistic conclusions. In particular, it is not helpful in understanding the politics of expertise in Congress. Consider the following illustration. The Office of Management and Budget (OMB), created in 1921 as the Bureau of the Budget, was originally designed as a neutral, expert source of information for the President. In its early days, the Bureau was by all accounts the very embodiment of neutral expertise. But under the influence of a succession of presidents starting with Franklin Roosevelt, the Bureau grew steadily more partisan and politically loyal. Now, as OMB, it has foregone any serious claim to neutrality and disinterestedness; it is an expert ally of the president. On the other hand, the Congressional Budget Office (CBO), intended as a legislative analogue to OMB, has experienced a nearly opposite history. After its creation in 1974, CBO devised a strategy for asserting neutrality and non-partisanship. By most accounts, it has grown less politicized over time, not more so.[18] By no means is CBO perfectly neutral, nor has it completely escaped charges of partisanship. But throughout much of its history, the agency has attempted to position itself publicly as a neutral policy expert, and few would doubt that it has developed a stronger claim of neutrality and bipartisanship than has OMB.

Similar contrasts between other parallel agencies are available. For example, in 1957, the Eisenhower administration created an office to provide expert advice on national security affairs and other issues, called the President's Science Advisory Committee (PSAC). Like OMB, PSAC was created with an aura of neutrality and technical objectivity. But that aura soon clashed with White House demands for loyalty, and PSAC ran afoul of a succession of presidents in the 1960s. In 1973, the Nixon administration abolished the office, because it had failed to demonstrate sufficient commitment to the President's policies. PSAC failed where OMB succeeded, because the former insisted on neutrality as a strategy, while the latter abandoned it.

Like OMB, PSAC also had a congressional analogue, intended by some to replicate the presidential office in the legislature: the Office of Technology Assessment. Just like CBO, this agency evolved since its creation in the direction of neutrality. It developed a strategy involving public professions of disinterestedness and non-partisanship. Rather than lead to its demise, this strategy contributed to a decade-long string of successes and praise from legislators and other policy experts.

These illustrations suggest that the politics of expertise is substantially more complicated than suggested by the traditional view of a secular trend toward politicization and the centralization of control over experts. Some experts grow more politicized over time and some less. In some cases, politicization appears functional for survival while in others it may be a recipe for organizational failure. The relationship between experts and politicians may evolve in several directions. What accounts for this fact?

The main argument of this book is that the answer lies in the nature of experts' relationships with politicians, and more specifically, in the institutional context of those relationships. Some institutional settings tend to elicit greater degrees of politicization from experts than others, regardless of the character of political decision-makers for whom the expertise is produced and regardless of the political inclinations of experts themselves. In debates over the desirability of politicians' attempts to evoke politicized or depoliticized expertise from subordinates, the influence of the larger institutional context of their relationships has received little attention. This book suggests that the character of the relationships between experts and politicians might be shaped more by institutional arrangements than the choices or styles of individual politicians and experts. This book argues that structure does indeed shape action, and despite the popularity of that construct in social science, it has generally been missed by students of policy analysis and the politics of expertise. Congress, I argue, shows how an institution with a highly pluralistic distribution of power tends to reward experts who provide broadly applicable, politically uncommitted expertise. In Congress, experts are likely to be sanctioned for displaying favoritism and rewarded for signaling neutrality. In the Executive Office of the President, by contrast, experts face a different set of incentives. They are likely to be sanctioned for displaying lack of commitment and rewarded for providing expertise designed to further a focused set of political interests.

One of this book's conclusions is that despite its reputation for being too highly politicized to be conducive to responsible policy expertise, Congress is actually quite successful at producing neutrally competent advisors. In fact it is better equipped than the executive branch to inform policy debates with balanced expert views.

THE OFFICE OF TECHNOLOGY ASSESSMENT

There are several ways that these matters might be examined empirically. For instance, one might survey policy-makers about informational needs, or examine the content of expert studies provided under different institutional arrangements. The approach used here is a case study, designed to detail the life cycle of an expertise-providing organization in Congress. The case analyzes the strategies adopted by a group of policy experts in response to demands for information placed on them by legislators.

The case is that of the Office of Technology Assessment, or OTA. Created in 1972, OTA was the product of congressional reorganization efforts of the early 1970s. It emerged out of two strands of reform: a desire to improve the content or "intelligence" of policy, as PSAC had done for the Eisenhower administration, and a desire to strengthen Congress' hand against the executive branch. Congress terminated OTA's operations in 1995, during the appropriations battles over implementing the Republican budget-balancing plan. The agency has the ignominious distinction of being the only congressional support office to have completed a cycle of birth and death.

OTA's work over two decades was not well known to the public, and there is almost no scholarly literature on the political logic of the agency's function in the legislature. But it developed a committed following on Capitol Hill that served as its internal constituency. One of its directors once commented jokingly that among congressional institutions, "OTA is larger only than the U.S. Botanic Gardens." The agency was the source of personnel for several high-level appointments in the Clinton administration, including John Gibbons, who left the position of agency head to become Assistant to the President for Science and Technology in 1993. As a Senator, Vice President Al Gore was one of the agency's chief patrons, and was responsible in large part for the transfer of personnel from OTA into the White House in 1993.

OTA's only formally stated mission was to provide expert analysis and information to Congress, and for this reason the organization provides a good focus for a study about the relationship between legislators and experts. Its technocratic title reflected the interest of some of the sponsors of its original authorizing legislation in scientific and technological matters, but the name grew to be something of a misnomer, because the agency provided expertise about policy problems of all kinds. While the agency was a cornerstone of the national science and technology policy network in Washington for over a decade, the bulk of its activities involved policy problems well beyond the confines of that policy area. Its studies addressed health care, energy policy, environmental issues, land and resource management, international trade, and defense. Nearly every committee of Congress occasionally relied on OTA for information, from the Budget and Appropriations Committees to Veterans Affairs.[19]

One of OTA's most visible and controversial contributions occurred on the day that the House passed the Brady Handgun Control Act of 1991, in one of the major legislative battles of the 102nd Congress. On the morning of the very close vote, *The New York Times* and *The Washington Post* both cited OTA in support of their editorial endorsements of the "Brady Bill" over the National Rifle Association's alternative bill. They wrote that the agency's research showed that the NRA's scheme was impractical and that the Brady Bill represented more sound policy. Interestingly enough, this kind of recognition by the nation's newspapers of record is a highly prized marker of influence at most Washington think tanks, but for reasons we will see, was not welcomed at the tiny OTA.

OTA's formally stated mission, providing objective analysis of policy problems, can obscure the politically dynamic role the agency played. It participated in the formulation of policy agendas, as legislators used its expertise to gauge the likely significance of policy problems. It was drawn into jurisdictional jockeying among committee chairs maneuvering for position and signaling one another of their intentions. The agency participated in oversight activities, when legislators used its expertise to review the claims and activities of executive agencies.

Matters of neutrality and the politicization of expert competence were in many ways the organizing principles of OTA's daily operations. The political environment in which OTA was to operate became clear even before the agency had begun operations. For instance, in the fall of 1973, when OTA's first appropriation was considered in Congress, the ranking Republican on the House Appropriations Committee, Elford Cederberg, opposed funding the agency and brought progress on establishing the agency to a halt. OTA's chief sponsor, Senator Edward Kennedy, stood in favor, and the two deadlocked the appropriations conference. Cederberg had opposed the idea of a new agency for Congress from the beginning, and portrayed OTA to his colleagues as a boondoggle by the ambitious Kennedy. After a number of futile efforts to out-maneuver Cederberg, Kennedy's office eventually devised a strategy for rescuing the agency from Cederberg's grasp. Kennedy staffers arranged for the appointment of J.M. Leathers, an executive of Dow Chemical, to an advisory committee set up to help steer OTA. Dow was an important corporate constituent in Cederberg's Michigan district, and when Leathers expressed his enthusiasm for serving on the committee—if OTA got off the ground—Cederberg capitulated and the conference approved the funding. Against a background like this, the agency struggled to find an operating strategy that would protect its annual appropriations and inoculate it against attacks like Cederberg's, and protect it against charges that it was manipulated by legislators like Kennedy.

My account of OTA's development of that strategy is not intended as an exhaustive documentation of the details of the agency's history. Although the essential outlines of the agency's life are presented here, I focus on the political logic of the agency's role in Congress, rather than on its internal stories. My interviews with congressional and agency personnel, as well as my examination of documentary materials, have been designed to illuminate the agency's interaction with legislators. To be sure, understanding this interaction requires an examination of how OTA organized itself internally, what processes of inquiry it used, and how it staffed itself. Where I have judged these matters important to understanding the politics of expertise in Congress, I discuss them here. Some topics that I do not examine closely are techniques of policy analysis employed by OTA staff, matters of its disciplinary mix of experts, incentives and career paths within the agency, and so on. I chose to include material on the politics of policy analysis rather than on policy analysis itself.

It is also not my intent to establish a general theory of the politics of expertise that applies to all cases and all circumstances. This work focuses on captive experts: those within the boundaries of political institutions. More specifically, it focuses on congressional support agencies, a feature of the legislature about which surprisingly little is known, and whose presence helps to distinguish Congress from most other legislatures. Private sector experts, and those in between—at quasi-governmental organizations—are beyond the scope of this study. They are indeed important, but I have left them for another time.

It is doubtful whether a single case study can fully substantiate a theory, and so some care must be taken in interpreting the evidence presented here. My intent is first to derive from some considerations of Congress a more satisfactory thesis about the politics of expert politicization than has been available. The second step in my approach is to explore that thesis through the case study, shedding light on its plausibility and implications.

To support the generalizability of my case study, I also provide mini-case studies of the other three congressional support agencies. If my account of the politics of expertise is sound, then it should also apply to the Congressional Research Service, the Congressional Budget Office, and the General Accounting Office. For the most part, these agencies are much better known than is OTA, and I rely mainly on secondary sources, supplemented with interviews, to test my explanation for these agencies.

The next chapter, chapter 2, develops an account of the politics of expertise and information. It returns to the illustrations of OMB and PSAC set out above, presents the standard account of expert politicization, and argues why it is inadequate. It then presents my own framework, based on assumptions and observations about the nature of politics and expertise.

Chapter 3 provides a descriptive overview of OTA and a brief look at some of the ways that legislators used the information the agency produced. It raises the issues of credibility and trust in the relationship between OTA and members of Congress. It shows that the utility of policy information from OTA was limited almost exclusively to one phase of the policy-making process. This chapter should be of interest to those who want a brief summary of OTA as an agency. Those already familiar with the agency or less interested in a descriptive portrait should turn their attention to the following chapter.

Chapter 4 describes the origins of OTA and explores its functions in the context of the system of separation of powers. It discusses the importance of congressional-executive relations in motivating legislators' demands for expertise from OTA. This chapter also provides a brief comparison of OTA to agencies in Europe that have been modeled after it, and points out distinctions that stem from differing institutional contexts. The chief claim of this chapter is that the goal of improving the content of policy through analysis is often inseparable from the institutional goal of maintaining congressional independence from the executive.

Chapter 5 explores the matter of neutrality and politicization. It examines OTA's development in the context of congressional partisanship, describing how OTA attempted to position itself in the face of competing policy demands from Republicans and Democrats. It describes the emergence of a strategy for responding to legislators' demands for control over the production of information, following the agency's near collapse in the late 1970s.

Chapter 6 continues the characterization of OTA's strategy for survival in the congressional environment, focusing on the committee system. It shows how heterogeneous demands for information from many committees reinforced OTA's choice of strategies for survival as an information agent.

Chapter 7 describes how OTA came to be abolished in 1995. It discusses how the agency became a target in efforts to balance the budget, and traces the rather remarkable appropriations cycle in which funding for the agency was eliminated.

Chapter 8 provides brief comparisons between OTA and the three other congressional agencies, the Congressional Budget Office, the Congressional Research Service, and the General Accounting Office. It shows how attempts by legislators to control information production have produced similar strategies for survival at these agencies. The comparison reinforces my conclusions about OTA, and suggests that the agency's experiences are indeed representative of a general pattern in Congress.

Chapter 9 provides concluding observations and draws lessons from the record of OTA as a case study in the politics of expertise.

Chapter 2

A *Theory of the Politicization of Expertise*

The matter of politicization lies just beneath the surface of nearly every discussion of expertise in politics, and it frequently emerges into the open in policy debates. Is the so-called expert advancing a political interest? Does a study of a policy problem come from disinterested analysts, or from advocates attempting to cloak themselves in the authority of science and expertise? Whose experts should be believed?

Such questions reveal a tension. The idealized image of the scientific expert involves not simply knowledge, but also a large element of objectivity, of being above politics and partisanship. The idealized policy expert brings the neutral authority of science to bear on politics. Experts derive legitimacy from their ability to appeal to non-political professional standards: the use of dispassionate scientific methods of inquiry, validation through peer review rather than mere assertion, and other classic elements of Mertonian science.[1]

At the same time, few observers believe any longer that this ideal is often realized in practice. Research in the sociology of science and scientific knowledge has dismantled Merton's model of a disinterested scientific elite. In its place is a scholarly theory of the contingent, socially constructed nature of science, where professional interest, gender, and other social factors shape the nature of expertise.[2] Public perceptions of expertise have paralleled this evolving scholarly view, developing from an extraordinary degree of trust in science after World War II to a much more skeptical and cautious contemporary attitude.

The dropping of the atomic bombs was in many ways the historical apex in the public image of science. For many in the U.S., the remarkable wartime technical successes—penicillin, radar, the bomb, and others—had demonstrated not just the ingenuity but the patriotism of America's technical elite. During the war, many had come to think of experts as an apolitical corps that could be trusted to help defeat the enemies and then turn its attention to improving life at home. As Roosevelt wrote in 1944 to Vannevar Bush, his wartime director of scientific research, the research experience gained by the thousands of scientists who had been mobilized for the war effort must be applied in the coming peacetime "for the improvement of national health, the creation of new enterprises bringing new jobs, and the betterment of the national standard of living."[3]

Indeed, at the war's end many expected something like a technical utopia, with the nation's corps of scientists and engineers producing a dazzling array of consumer goods, conveniences, and improvements in health and the quality of life. In this optimism, little attention was paid to the obvious political matters: the costs of committing resources in a particular way, the creation of losers as well as winners in the process of social change, market externalities and the need for regulatory regimes, and so on. The benefits would flow not just from hardware, but from benevolent scientific judgments about social goals that everyone could agree upon.

It did not take long after the war's end for the heroic image of science to be burst. One of the first blows landed in the midst of the anti-communist hysteria, which came to point fingers at scientists too. Within a decade of the war's end, Robert Oppenheimer, wartime director of the Los Alamos laboratory and former head of the Institute for Advanced Study, had been publicly defrocked over allegations of his being a security risk. The charges were almost certainly groundless, but they drove home the point that scientists just might have politics after all. Perhaps more than any other, that episode symbolized the beginning of the end of wartime scientific *esprit de corps* in the United States.

The naiveté behind that idealized image of technical experts also eroded in the face of policy debates that revealed political fault lines within the scientific community. Environmental struggles of the 1960s and 70s showed that the nation's scientific corps was divided into proponents and opponents of various industrial and commercial activities with environmental and social costs. Battles over the use of pesticides, clean air and clean water regulations, nuclear power, the Supersonic Transport, and other issues revealed a sometimes highly fractious scientific community. In the same period, the consumer movement and the war in Vietnam produced more public rifts among experts, making abundantly clear the point that scientists, engineers, and other experts on public issues had values and political interests that shaped their ostensibly neutral, technical contributions to politics.

A public more jaded with technical claims, whether about the feasibility of Ronald Reagan's Strategic Defense Initiative, the risks of exposure to cigarette smoke, or the effects of health care reform, is now given to question the neutrality and objectivity of policy experts and those who repeat their claims. While the cachet of science remains strong, few still trust its practitioners to adhere to the truly objective, benevolent ideal type. The contemporary skepticism among scholars and the public about technical expertise reveals the underlying tension in the politics of expert participation in politics. On the one hand, acknowledging that an "expert" is in fact expert requires accepting the availability of a technical standard of knowledge. In politics, to use the label "expert" or "scientist" is to acknowledge the legitimacy of the scientific ideal type. To distinguish between the expert and the non-expert, or between the expert and the mere advocate, is to accept a greater claim on the part of the former to adherence to the methods and goal of objectivity.

On the other hand, over the past thirty years participants in politics—like the scholarly community—have increasingly acknowledged that experts may bring interests, values, and political views to the policy process, and that these limit the fulfillment of the goal of objectivity.

The conclusion to be drawn is that "objectivity" should be approached as a matter of degree. Experts can be more or less objective, more or less neutral, more or less credible as experts rather than simply advocates. Without some claim to standards of professional neutrality the policy expert is little more than a highly informed advocate, yet absolute neutrality is an ideal not often achieved. Much of the politics of expertise is played out in this terrain between the inherently interested process of advocacy at one end, and the ideal notion of disinterested expertise at the other.

For the purpose of studying expertise, it is necessary to have a method for referring to experts' location on this spectrum. I use the term "degree of politicization" for that purpose. The term refers to the extent to which expertise provided by an individual or organization is shaded by political orientation. Experts with a high degree of politicization show a pattern of political allegiance. This allegiance is the source of what is commonly called "bias." Bias may be liberal or conservative in orientation, or may be parochial in nature, through loyalty to a particular position on a policy question or to some institutional or other interest. The idealized, objective expert is one with a low degree of politicization, while the informed advocate has a high degree.

Degree of politicization is not a quantitative measure, but rather serves as qualitative descriptor of experts' political orientation. It can be difficult to measure with precision, but has several indicators. A high degree of politicization is often associated with correspondence between experts' agendas and the political agendas of a specific interest or group of interests. It is also marked by patterns in the political implications of experts' work. The results of experts' studies sometimes become predictable in their support for a particular political or institutional position. The Office of Management and Budget, for instance, which was originally designed as a neutral reservoir of expertise, is now anything but depoliticized. The National Academy of Sciences, on the other hand, has developed a reputation for independence and political disinterestedness.

Differences in degree of politicization are also evident in private research institutes. Think tanks providing policy expertise to the national government are distributed across the political landscape and vary widely in their degree of politicization. Many, such as the Brookings Institution and RAND, publicly state a commitment to political disinterestedness and a low degree of politicization, and take great pains to nurture the perception of their position on the spectrum of politicization.[4] Others signal that they are politicized. The Institute for Policy Studies, for instance, proclaims itself allied with the political left, while the Heritage Foundation, the American Enterprise Institute, and the Cato Institute explicitly advertise themselves as conservative in orientation.[5]

The degree of politicization of experts is a central facet of their place in politics. The claims of highly politicized experts are sometimes discounted by opponents at the same time they are sought out by those with allied interests. Experts who can lay claim to a low degree of politicization often earn the widest credibility, but may be less sought after than those offering strong advocacy along with their analysis.

In this study my chief interest is in exploring trends in degree of politicization. What factors lead to relatively high degrees of politicization on the part of some experts and relatively low degrees in others? What explains variation in experts' strategies?

To make this problem tractable, I have focused on explaining politicization on the part of what I call captive experts: organizations a) whose chief function is providing expert information, and b) which are embedded within the institutions of government. I therefore exclude independent think tanks, nongovernmental and quasi-governmental research organizations, universities, and the like. Such disparate sources of expertise exist in complex and often unique social and institutional contexts, and so they do not hold much promise as a starting point for untangling relationships and trends. To be sure, institutional experts also may respond to a complex set of factors, but their immediate political environments are typically more readily characterized: their missions and primary patrons are often more easily identifiable, and their source of funding and the authority relationships that follow are more stable and traceable.

THE STANDARD ACCOUNT OF EXPERT POLITICIZATION

The best extant explanation of the degree of politicization of captive policy expertise might be deemed the standard account of expert politicization. In practice, it is not so much a formally stated theory as a collection of observations. In this view, expertise located in government institutions is believed to exhibit a secular trend toward greater politicization. Some political leaders, like Richard Nixon and Ronald Reagan, exhibited stronger preferences for politicized expertise, while others, like Jimmy Carter, revealed less strong preferences. But short-term variations in preferences notwithstanding, the predictable pattern is that of expert sources of information within political institutions growing more politicized. The result is the ascendance of politicized advice, constructed and presented with advocacy in mind.

This characteristic pattern is sometimes described in terms of the decay of "neutral competence," a term introduced into the study of public administration by Kaufman forty years ago.[6] In the literature, the term typically is applied to the subject of presidential organization, but is descriptive of a larger quality of the relationship between politicians on the one hand, and subordinate experts and administrators on the other.[7] Heclo describes the ideally neutral expert as providing information and expertise to political decision-makers in a politically "uncommitted" way.[8] The neutrally expert organization places primary emphasis on the substance of policy problems, and only secondarily on the political impact of policy choices—"politics" in a narrow sense of the word. The neutrally competent expert is different from the political advisor; the neutral expert can supply expertise and judgment for a series of political leaders with different goals, different values, different partisan objectives. The political advisor, expert as he or she may be, is not so politically uncommitted. The ideal of the neutral expert providing uncommitted assistance to politicians was one cornerstone of the Progressive belief that administration could be separated from politics. The neutral expert is definitive of a low degree of politicization.

The standard account consists essentially of the claim that neutrally expert organizations tend to evolve in the direction of greater politicization. Because politics cannot be cleanly separated from administration or the application of policy expertise, experts who pursue the ideal of objectivity cannot exist in a state of equilibrium with their political patrons—they develop into providers of "responsive" competence or expertise.

The reason for the evolution from low to high politicization is straightforward in this view: politicians do not want neutral experts, they want politically committed, loyal experts who share their policy objectives. Neutral competence is insufficient for political leaders, and can even be an impediment to governance by insulating policy organizations from central political control. Neutral expertise in government can contribute to fragmentation and conflict among agencies.[9] In short, it may reduce the political responsiveness of institutions to central political impulses.

Instead of neutral-tending expertise, policy-makers seek expertise that is responsive to political needs, that is designed to help overcome obstacles to the exercise of power, especially in the case of the presidency.[10] As Rourke writes, political leaders want "passionate commitment rather than passive neutrality."[11] For this reason, they attempt to convert neutrally expert organizations into more politicized providers of information.

Moe identifies two tactics pursued by presidents seeking to increase the degree of politicization on the part of expert advisors and administrators: centralization of policy-making authority within the White House, and politicization of administrative arrangements.[12] Presidents draw decisions into the White House, where they can count on the greatest possible loyalty and responsiveness from staff. At the same time, they use their power of appointment to place loyalists as far out into the bureaucracy as possible. These tactics work to undermine neutral competence and promote responsive competence.

Two examples introduced in the first chapter illustrate what appears to be the predictive power of this account of the politics of expertise. The first example has become a classic case: the Bureau of the Budget (BOB), created by the Budget and Accounting Act of 1921. The Bureau was designed to be an "impartial, expert, professional organization" that had "nothing to do with politics."[13] Its focus was to be efficiency and economy, and it represented a classic Progressive attempt at separating politics from administration. The Bureau may never have represented the full realization of those goals, but the idea of neutral competence was an important standard, and, as Heclo writes, the concept "took root" at BOB in the organization's early years.[14] The ideal of the neutral expert was institutionalized in the agency's structure and processes over the first decade of its existence.[15]

By the time Franklin Roosevelt assumed office, BOB's orientation toward neutral competence had become entrenched. But Roosevelt needed a responsive and committed set of presidential institutions equal to the policy tasks he was pursuing. The Brownlow reforms of 1939, including the creation of the Executive Office of the President (EOP), laid the foundation for a more responsive and committed presidency, and drew BOB a step closer to the president. Truman, Eisenhower, Kennedy, Johnson, and Nixon built in succession upon this foundation, expanding the use of appointments to place loyalists, creating new policy offices within the EOP such as the Council of Economic Advisors, and, in 1970, converting BOB into the Office of Management and Budget (OMB), complete with a new layer of political appointees intended to enhance the office's responsiveness and counter its tendency for insulation.[16] By the time of Nixon's resignation in 1974 after Watergate, the presidency, and BOB/OMB along with it, had been remade into a set of political institutions tuned to facilitating the exercise of power by the president. Neutral competence, both as a standard and as a matter of practice, was all but gone. Although the period 1975–1981—the Ford and Carter years— was largely a time of status quo in presidential institution-building, subsequent presidents have continued to build OMB as an instrument of policymaking. Its evolution from low to high politicization was complete by the time of David Stockman's tenure at the office.[17]

The second illustration of the standard account comes from a much less well-known agency, the President's Science Advisory Committee (PSAC), and it illustrates the effect of experts' attempts to resist efforts at politicization. PSAC emerged during the Eisenhower administration in 1957, and was dismantled by the Nixon White House in 1973. Whereas BOB/ OMB successfully converted from low to high politicization in response to presidents' demands, PSAC failed to make that evolution, lost the support of its political patrons, and failed to survive.

PSAC, which was led by the Special Assistant to the President for Science and Technology, was created during the crisis atmosphere in the United States following the Sputnik launch. The idea for such an office within the White House came from the Office of Defense Mobilization's Science Advisory Committee, which conducted a series of discussions in 1957 with the Eisenhower administration about creating a venue for high-level technical advice to the president. The idea of an office modelled on the Council of Economic Advisors appealed to Eisenhower. His announcement of the creation of PSAC in November 1957 served as a mechanism for reassuring the public that U.S. military and technical leadership was secure, and for quieting critics of the administration's response to Soviet accomplishments in space.[18]

PSAC, directed first by James Killian as Special Assistant to the President, quickly developed into more than White House window dressing. The office served as a point of liaison between the administration and prominent scientists (and a few engineers) around the country interested in defense and space policy. Its work on anti-ballistic missiles, arms control, basic research and graduate education, life and food sciences, high energy physics, and other technical policy issues made it a prominent advisory apparatus in the Eisenhower White House.

Killian's successor, George Kistiakowsky, developed an even stronger personal relationship with the president, and proved a powerful counterbalance to the Department of Defense in policy discussions.[19] The influence of PSAC and the "science adviser" continued during the Kennedy years, and led one administration critic, Senator Stuart Symington of Missouri, to call Jerome Wiesner, the first PSAC chair for President Kennedy, "the most dangerous man in government."[20] The period between 1957 and 1963 is commonly recalled as the "golden days" or "glory days" of the office; it provided candid advice to the White House under conditions of low politicization that approximated the neutral competence ideal. Killian reports that the office saw itself as a communications center for technical advice unshaped by political agendas or partisanship.[21] PSAC enjoyed substantial credibility, derived from the perception that it represented the best available technical expertise, presented neutrally and objectively to presidents who would listen.

Yet the inherent contradiction in PSAC's mission as a neutral player in the White House produced strains even by the end of the Kennedy administration, just six years after the office's creation. PSAC staff found that adhering to ideals of objectivity raised questions about their loyalty and fitness to serve the White House, while too close an adherence to political interests undermined their credibility as an apolitical technical elite. Cracks in the relationship widened when Johnson assumed office. Johnson's well-known mistrust of the intellectuals he inherited from Kennedy extended to PSAC. Moreover, he had specific disputes with the office over space policy and escalation of the war in Vietnam. His advisors' antipathy for his policies guaranteed their exclusion from decision-making; PSAC's fall from grace was precipitous. By 1966, Johnson's science advisor and head of PSAC was concerned that his office was essentially superfluous; it had attempted to remain aloof and politically independent in its advising, and continually earned itself a back seat to more politically loyal White House advisers like McGeorge Bundy and Robert MacNamara, and under Nixon, Henry Kissinger.

The unwillingness of policy experts at PSAC to become politically responsive to the president continued after the election of 1968, and their doom was essentially guaranteed in the Nixon White House. Nixon was unhappy with PSAC's opposition to the Vietnam War, to anti-ballistic missile defense, and to the Supersonic Transport. Kissinger fed President Nixon's fears that the scientists were not sufficiently loyal politically, and after some cases of present and former PSAC members' going public with their opposition to administration policies, Nixon abolished the office in January 1973. The experiment in neutral competence had lasted only a decade and a half. PSAC was criticized at the time for "viewing its role more as a national adviser than as part of the president's family."[22] As one PSAC member in the Nixon administration himself later acknowledged, the office "did not work within the President's agenda," and tended to "meddle in the affairs of the departments and agencies rather than assisting the White House in accomplishing its goals."[23] PSAC had insisted on a low degree of politicization, and once its immediate mission of bolstering U.S. efforts in the space and missile race of the late 1950s and early 1960s had played itself out, its strategy made it incompatible with White House politics.[24]

CONSTRUCTING A NEW ACCOUNT OF
THE POLITICS OF EXPERTISE

These two cases, PSAC and BOB/OMB, illustrate in different ways the standard account of expert politicization: political principals want responsiveness from their expert agents; those agents' likelihood of surviving is a function of how well they adapt by evolving in the direction of high politicization.

This explanation of the degree of politicization of institutional experts appears to have the ring of simple truth. Even the most naive observer of politics expects advisors to presidents, senators, and agency heads to be "biased" in favor of their bosses. But the simplicity of this theory is also its downfall—it merely predicts that degree of politicization increases with time, and cannot speak to cases where expert organizations might grow less politicized over time, or where agencies might exhibit different degrees of politicization. The Office of Technology Assessment (OTA), created explicitly as an analogue to PSAC for Congress, was highly politicized in its first half-dozen years of operation. It was widely viewed as dedicated to a narrow set of political interests, and its technical credibility suffered as a result. But OTA evolved over time to be *less politicized;* it became less partisan, less parochial, and more credible as a neutral provider of expertise. The agency exhibited an unmistakable trend from high toward lower politicization. As we will see later, other agencies in Congress have exhibited a similar pattern of development. The standard account of the politics of expertise is at a loss to explain cases such as this.

Moreover, in its focus on explaining executive organization, the standard view inherits a larger problem in the study of the presidency, namely too great a focus on individuals and their styles. The relationship between presidents and their advisors, which has received a significant amount of scholarly attention, is just one instance of the general class of relationships between politicians and experts of all kinds. When considering that larger class, the issue that stands out most sharply is the need to examine the influence of different institutional arrangements. Indeed, it may be that differentiating between institutions with different structures, different arrangements of power, and different constituencies could tell us more about the politics of expertise than comparing the differing tastes in advisers of individual politicians such as Eisenhower and Nixon.

If observers of politics have learned anything over the last two decades, it is that institutions do matter. Institutional arrangements vary, and as they do, so vary the ways that political demands are aggregated and policy produced. An improved account of the politics of expertise should explain variation in expert politicization, and a good place to start is by looking at institutional context.

In constructing an improved account, it is useful to begin with three considerations: the nature of politicians' needs for information, the strategies of experts in responding to those needs, and the role of institutions in mediating the interaction of the two. One should be clear about assumptions and observations regarding these issues because they are so often passed over in discussions of the politics of expertise.

What is the nature of politicians' needs for information? A simple assumption about the nature of politics itself is in order as a starting point. It should be assumed that politics is not a search for knowledge, but a search for power. That is, the primary object of politics is not the discovery of knowledge, but the instrumental use of knowledge, along with other resources, in the pursuit of various goals.

This assumption is important because it focuses attention on the fact that political actors can be expected to use information to the extent that it enhances their power. Political leaders need expert information about policy for many reasons: in pursuit of reelection, in pursuit of the making of policy, in pursuit of prestige and influence. Regardless of specific goals, their interest in expertise is tied to its instrumentality, its capacity to further some purpose.

That political actors should be, above all, political, may seem pedestrian and even tautological. Yet observers of politics, as well as participants themselves, often find it tempting to criticize the so-called "political use" of expertise. It is common to hear complaints about the selective use of information. These criticisms appeal implicitly to an ideal standard of the value of knowledge for knowledge's sake; this standard is inappropriate to the political arena.

This assumption is a reminder that the practice of politics is not the same as the practice of science, even when science is invoked in politics. We might hold experts themselves to objective rules of evidence in presenting information, but should not do quite the same with political actors. We should not expect policy-makers to expend resources acquiring information about problems not connected directly to their power and political objectives. Policy expertise, like money or political organization, is a resource for legislators, to be invested toward a political return. Unlike the researcher or analyst, the politician does not seek knowledge in order to know, but in order to do. This assumption suggests that we should expect to find political actors using their power to reward expertise that helps them, sanctioning expertise that hurts them, and that we should find them indifferent to expertise that does not hold the potential to help or hurt.

What of experts themselves? In addition to the pursuit of knowledge, it is important to recognize that they share more pragmatic goals with other bureaucrats and administrators. Experts too have institutional interests at stake in the policy process. It should be acknowledged that they are just as cognizant of how their advice will shape their own fortunes as how it will shape public policy.

Organizations of experts should be assumed to behave according to an incentive common to other bureaucratic agents. They seek to ensure their own survival against the encroachment of rivals and against threats to their budgets and jurisdiction. Their provision of expertise is aimed toward building constituencies for themselves upon whom they can draw political support. They avoid making enemies who can harm them, and they solicit the friendship of powerful patrons. This is to say that expertise-providing organizations can be expected to adopt survival strategies tailored to the demands of their environment. Institutional experts can be expected to devise strategies that maximize their chances of political survival and their influence, while minimizing threats. This assumption too may seem pedestrian, but is important for focusing attention away from expertise and information itself and onto those who produce it.

A final consideration concerns institutional arrangements and how these might be expected to link the pursuits of politicians and those of the experts who support them. The aggregation and expression of political actors' preferences, and their ability to apply resources to pursuing their interests, is shaped by institutional surroundings. Their ability to wield power, to impose sanctions, and to distribute benefits and rewards is shaped by the structure of their environment.

There exists a nearly infinite variety of institutional structures, from those approximating the Weberian bureaucratic ideal to loosely structured organizations with porous boundaries and flexible or shifting lines of internal authority. In this study, I focus on the degree of centralization of authority as one of the most important dimensions of institutional variation. By a high degree of centralization I mean institutions where power is consolidated in the hands of a few leaders or managers at the top of a hierarchy, while by low degree of centralization I refer to those where power is distributed among those located further down an institutional hierarchy.

Changes in degree of centralization have been a defining feature of

Congress. Much of the twentieth-century history of power inside the legislature is one of decreasing centralization. In the years after the "Revolution of 1910," power in the House flowed from the speakership downward to the committees, and then after the decentralizing reforms of the 1970s, from the committee barons downward to the subcommittees. During the 104th Congress, power shifted back toward the speakership in the House. Degree of decentralization is a potentially useful yardstick for comparing Congress and other institutions.

Because political goals and power are more highly focused in more centralized institutions, expressions of demand for policy expertise are also likely to be more focused. Conversely, power in decentralized institutions tends to be more pluralistic in nature, and expressed political objectives more heterogeneous, so the expression of demands for policy expertise should parallel this heterogeneity in political goals.

What do these brief considerations about politicians, experts, and institutions lead one to expect regarding the problem of interest here, degree of politicization of expertise? At the very least, we should expect institutional arrangements to structure the market in which experts and politicians conduct their commerce. More specifically, these considerations lead one to expect experts located in more centralized institutions to adopt different strategies than those in less centralized institutions. Experts in more centralized institutions should tend to provide expertise that supports a more focused set of political objectives, while those in more decentralized institutional contexts should provide expertise that supports a wide variety of political objectives.

So a link should be expected between the degree of politicization of expertise and the degree of centralization of power in an institution. The greater the centralization of power in an institution, the greater the degree of politicization of supporting expertise. Conversely, the lower the degree of centralization of power, the lower the degree of politicization of supporting expertise.

This is to say something which is quite simple, but which has largely escaped the notice of those concerned with promoting depoliticized expertise in government. *The degree of politicization of expertise may be more an institutional phenomenon than a product of the preferences or style of politicians, the moral or professional commitment of experts, or an inexorable trend away from neutrality.* In the traditional view of expertise, the way toward the normatively attractive goal of neutral competence in government lies in the motives and styles of politicians, and in exhortation and the professional socialization of experts. Ultimately, though, the best one can hope for is to attempt to slow the inevitable tainting of experts by politics. If the view suggested here is right, the way lies in the design of political structures and the incentives to which experts respond, and there is no reason to believe it impossible for balanced, neutral-tending experts to exist inside some political institutions.

To return to Congress, what does this view suggest about the provision of expertise inside the legislature? Because the modern Congress is highly decentralized in comparison to institutions of the executive branch, we should expect to find Congress tending to elicit comparatively depoliticized expertise. We should even expect to find the *opposite* of a secular trend toward politicization. In Congress, power is shared, albeit unequally, between members of two parties, who in some years have divided control of the two chambers. The committee system further divides power, distributing it among many committee chairs and scores of subcommittee chairs. Traditionally, weak leadership and party structure (except in the House beginning in 1995) further distribute power.

Congressional fragmentation and pluralism of interests should elicit from experts operating strategies that are much less politicized than those typically taken by executive branch experts. As experts attempt to meet Congress' collective demands for information, they should find themselves responding to heterogeneous political and policy interests. They should be attuned to fulfilling the demands of competing power centers—in the committees and subcommittees, in the parties and leadership structures, and among the many members themselves. This is not to say that any expert can fulfill the ideal of objectivity. It is not to say that one should expect all experts in the executive branch to be hopelessly politicized and all those in Congress to be models of objectivity. And it is not to say that individual experts will not privately have their own predilections, values, and even ideologies. Rather, we should expect to find differing institutional contexts producing divergent trends. In Congress, we should expect to find a low degree of politicization functional for survival. The primary emphasis of the evaluation of OTA that follows is an exploration of this idea.

Chapter 3

OTA: "The Office of WHAT?"

One of the most striking features of the Office of Technology Assessment was its unassuming character as an organization. The agency was one of a few islands of informality and unceremoniousness in a city known for ceremony and the formal trappings of power. Hierarchical control and bureaucratic procedure were kept at a minimum at OTA. Dress was casual—there were few suits in this Washington office, except on occasions where an analyst testified in a hearing or met with legislators. The style of the agency's longest serving director, John Gibbons, reflected the tenor of the agency. Managers and analysts alike addressed him as "Jack," and he was one of the few agency heads in government who could sometimes be seen without a coat or tie.

The agency's informal culture was reflected in its physical facilities. Inside, OTA looked more like a university than a government office, with unassuming rooms and hallways that lacked both the bureaucratic appearance of some government buildings and the grandness of others. For most of its two decades, the agency leased space in a nondescript red brick office building that appeared somewhat out of place in Washington. The address, 600 Pennsylvania Avenue, sounded prestigious until one encountered the SE designation, for "Southeast," which placed OTA beyond Capitol Hill and the Library of Congress buildings. It was the last government office on Pennsylvania Avenue before one left official Washington and entered the city's poorest and most crime-ridden section. OTA was well away from the centers of power that run from the Capitol building west and northwest.

The agency's location and demeanor were symbolic of its strategy for acceptance in Congress. The informality and physical remove from the main corridors of influence reflected cautiousness about being viewed as a broker of power or as being allied with political interests or policy positions. While serving as director, Gibbons often expressed the view that OTA's job was to provide analysis of technical problems and policy options, while it had to be left to legislators to make choices among options. His claims about the possibility of clearly separating normative and analytic judgements may appear somewhat optimistic, but this view became something of an organizing principle at OTA. As we will see later, the centerpiece of the agency's strategy for survival in an institution with many competing interests and no single center of power was the strenuous avoidance of political judgments and policy advocacy.

MISSION AND STRUCTURE

OTA was created by the Technology Assessment Act of 1972, which assigned the agency a mission of providing neutral, competent assessments about the probable beneficial and harmful effects of new technologies. The agency's sponsor in the House during the late 1960s, Rep. Emilio Daddario, explains that his view at the time was that OTA would serve to help members "minimize the negative effects of new technologies and maximize the positive effects."[1] Daddario's perspective is reflected in the legislative language, which indicates that "it is essential that, to the fullest extent possible, the consequences of technological applications be anticipated, understood, and considered in determination of public policy on existing and emerging national problems."[2] In this rather technocratic formulation, the agency's contribution was to be improved foresight about the consequences of political decisions involving scientific or technological questions.

The idea for an office dedicated to such issues emerged from a group of "science advice" advocates in Washington during the mid-1960s, and found its way into Congress through Daddario, who then chaired the Subcommittee on Science, Research and Technology of the House Committee on Science and Technology. Harvey Brooks of Harvard, Jerome Wiesner of MIT, and other veterans of the creation of PSAC in the White House turned their interest in science and government to Congress. Flushed with what appeared to some to be the PSAC success, this group of science advocates was hopeful that they might next outfit Congress with technical expertise.

At the same time, a broader "technology assessment" movement was taking hold in some parts of academia, reflecting a belief that "rationalist thinking and futurist techniques could be combined to anticipate the impacts of technology and steer a course toward better use of resources."[3] Proponents of technology assessment argued that some part of the solution to political problems posed by technology could be found in what was essentially more technology—analytic modeling of sociotechnical change.

Growing environmental concerns in the United States, demands for the restraint of military technology in light of the war in Vietnam, and a general sense that technology might somehow be "out of control" gave salience to this academic interest in improving the intelligence of government. Many beyond the northeast corridor of scholars were questioning whether Congress was up to the challenges of dealing with effects of the new technologies that seemed to present such dramatic issues.[4] An outpouring of books intended for both public and academic audiences contributed momentum to the movement for introspection about the effects of technology. Between 1962 and 1969, Rachel Carson's *Silent Spring*, Jacques Ellul's *The Technological Society*, Herbert Marcuse's *One Dimensional Man*, Leo Marx's *The Machine in the Garden*, Theodore Roszak's *The Making of a Counter Culture*, and others, all suggested in one way or another that the nation was often failing to make informed choices about the use of science and technology.

To some legislators like Emilio Daddario, the message was clear: it was incumbent upon Congress to upgrade its own ability to make wise choices. In the House, Daddario held hearings on the use of technology assessment, investigating how the success that "science advice" had enjoyed for a few years in the White House might be brought to Congress.[5] The subcommittee issued a preliminary report in 1966, and held a series of discussions throughout the late 1960s. Daddario commissioned reports by four groups, the Legislative Reference Service,[6] the National Academy of Sciences, the National Academy of Engineering, and the National Academy of Public Administration. The National Academy of Sciences report, the most scholarly of the four, eventually became a classic for its inquiry into the process of technological development and the nature of decision-making about technology.[7]

After discussions over the span of several years, the subcommittee was ready to proceed with legislation establishing an office for assessing technology by 1970. Daddario attempted to attach an amendment for that purpose to the Legislative Reorganization Act of 1970, but was ruled out of order on the floor because his proposal called for presidential appointments to the agency's board. The next year, the House Science Committee reported Daddario's bill and it was taken up again on the floor, where it passed with several modifications.

The bill, much of which had been drafted by Harvey Brooks, called for an agency to be constituted around a board of directors comprised of legislators, private citizens, the head of the Congressional Research Service (the

Legislative Reference Service prior to the 1970 reorganization act), and the Comptroller General. An amendment by Rep. Jack Brooks, who feared too much influence might accrue to those on the board from outside the legislature, dropped non-congressional membership on the board, leaving a body of twelve legislators to control the new agency. Brooks used an old phrase to describe to his colleagues what he felt the relationship between experts and politicians should be, saying he wanted the experts to be "on tap, not on top."[8]

Some members worried that the proposed organization might grow to become too powerful, possibly challenging the authority of the committee chairs as gatekeepers to policy expertise. Rep. Charles Mosher led an effort to inoculate against an accretion of power. He modified the OTA bill so that control over the agency would rest strictly in the hands of committee chairs. That way the agency could not be used by junior members to challenge the committees' prerogatives; nor could it develop too much independence. These institutional reins meant that only chairs of full committees, acting alone or on behalf of the committee or ranking minority member, could request a study from the agency. Control over its resources would be off limits to the rest of Congress. This arrangement was important not only because it contributed in a small way toward the preservation of committee power in an era of decentralization, but because it eventually overlaid jurisdictional tensions between committees on the agency. The limits on the size of the agency's clientele also would become a factor in the agency's demise much later, in the 104th Congress.

Mosher also wanted to be sure that the agency would act only as a clearinghouse for outside expertise and would not itself become a locus of policy information. He sought to prevent agency staff from themselves performing "technology assessments," wanting them instead to act as brokers of expertise from universities and elsewhere. This too was intended to prevent an accumulation of power. As a result, OTA was provided authorization to hire outside contractors to contribute to studies, although the legislation did not explicitly prohibit the agency from developing technical expertise of its own. Eventually, as the agency grew, legislators and agency staff found it necessary for OTA to acquire its own expertise within the agency, and legislators dropped their concerns about OTA's overstepping its bounds in this way.

When the OTA legislation was taken up in the Senate in March 1972, it was championed by Senator Edward Kennedy, who shared some of Daddario's enthusiasm for technical issues and who steered the bill through a relatively uncontroversial voice vote, skirmishing with only a few colleagues over the new agency. Before passing the bill, Senators added language guaranteeing equal representation for both parties on the board of directors, which was to be known as the Technology Assessment Board, or TAB, and they created an advisory council for the board. This council, known as the Technology Assessment Advisory Council, or TAAC, was to be composed of members from outside Congress, to serve as a form of replacement for the non-congressional board positions that had been removed in the House. The Council's mission was to advise congressional board members, and to serve as a form of public liaison for OTA.[9] The House agreed to a conference report on October 4, and President Nixon signed the act creating OTA into law on October 13, 1972.

Because the law passed too late for an initial fiscal year 1973 appropriation, the new agency had to wait more than a year for funds, which eventually came in late 1973 in the supplemental appropriations bill over which Kennedy and Elford Cederberg tangled in conference. The agency became operational in early 1974, the year that Nixon left office, and it joined Congress' two existing support agencies, the Congressional Research Service (CRS), and the General Accounting Office (GAO). The new agency's operations were expected to be more like those of GAO than CRS. It would undertake in-depth studies of policy problems, which it would publish in comprehensive reports. These studies would provide expert judgment and "assessment" of questions posed by committees, rather than convey the kind of factual reference, data compilation, or brief issue summaries being provided by CRS.

THE DIRECTOR AND BOARD

The board of directors that emerged from the House and Senate deliberations proved to be a fundamental influence on the operation and institutionalization of the agency. The arrangement was unique; no other congressional agency was directed by a board. OTA board members were appointed by the Speaker and Senate President pro tempore, on the recommendations of the majority and minority leaders of each chamber. In addition to stipulating equal representation between parties, OTA's authorizing legislation also provided that the position of board chair and vice-chair would rotate between chambers. In practice, the board observed a tradition of giving the chair to a member of the majority party in the chamber to which the position was assigned. Legislators who led the agency's board since 1974 are listed in Table 1.

As this roster shows, the leadership of OTA's board was a restricted club, despite the provisions for rotation. Senators Kennedy and Stevens, and Representatives Brown and Udall were among the agency's most highly in-

Table 1. CHAIRS OF OTA BOARD OF DIRECTORS

Congress	Chair	Vice Chair
103rd	Sen. Edward Kennedy-D	Rep. Don Sundquist-R
102nd	Rep. George Brown-D	Sen. Ted Stevens-R
101st	Sen. Edward Kennedy-D	Rep. Clarence Miller-R
100th	Rep. Morris Udall-D	Sen. Ted Stevens-R
99th	Sen. Ted Stevens-R	Rep. Morris Udall-D
98th	Rep. Morris Udall-D	Sen. Ted Stevens-R
97th	Sen. Ted Stevens-R	Rep. Morris Udall-D
96th	Rep. Morris Udall-D	Sen. Ted Stevens-R
95th	Sen. Edward Kennedy-D	Rep. Larry Winn, Jr.-R
94th	Rep. Olin Teague-D	Sen. Clifford Case-R
93rd	Sen. Edward Kennedy-D	Rep. Charles A. Mosher-R

volved board members over the years, as was Rep. John Dingell in later years, although he never served as chair.

The board's most important function was to shape the agency's agenda. The board approved each study before it was begun, and it also authorized release of studies after they were completed. Board members therefore acted as a second level of gatekeeping control, after the committee chairs who were authorized to request studies. In this sense, the board's influence extended beyond policy-setting for OTA, as a corporate board might set policy for a private firm. The board did not change the substantive findings of OTA analysts, but sometimes insisted on rewording or repackaging of conclusions, or on the softening of language members found too pointed. The board withheld only one study in the agency's entire history because of disagreements over its content. While all OTA studies contained disclaimers that the contents did not necessarily represent the views of members of the board, the board gave its collective approval to the release of every report.

In addition to exerting influence on what OTA did, the board also served as a two-way conduit between Congress and the agency. It provided a channel for congressional interests and concerns into the agency, helping make it responsive to legislators' interests. Members of Congress often used their colleagues on the board to press issues with the agency.

The board also represented agency interests to Congress. Board members assisted the agency in its annual appropriations process. Board members often served as protective guardians for OTA. One of their most frequent forms of aid involved the prevention of legislative mandates. Legislators occasionally tried to circumvent the normal study request process through committee chairs by inserting language in bills to require OTA studies. When these mandates passed, OTA was directed by law to undertake the

Table 2. OTA BOARD OF DIRECTORS 103rd CONGRESS*

Sen. Edward Kennedy, Chair
Rep. Don Sundquist, Vice Chair

Sen. Ernest Hollings	Rep. George Brown, Jr.
Sen. Claiborne Pell	Rep. John Dingell
Sen. Orrin Hatch	Rep. Amo Houghton
Sen. Charles Grassley	Rep. Michael Oxley
Sen. David Durenburger	Rep. Jim McDermott

Dr. Roger Herdman, OTA Director
(non-voting member)

*In the 104th Congress, the House leadership did not appoint board members, because the agency's future was uncertain from the outset. From the Senate, Kennedy, Hollings, Pell, Hatch, and Grassley served as an acting board through the end of fiscal year 1995. (Durenberger did not return to the Senate.)

When these mandates passed, OTA was directed by law to undertake the studies regardless of its commitment of resources in other areas—a situation the agency tried assiduously to avoid.

For instance, the Americans with Disabilities Act of 1990 mandated an OTA study on accessibility of public transportation systems for persons with disabilities. From the perspective of the agency, mandates such as this wrought havoc on budget and work plans, and often took the organization into areas where it had little expertise. Because OTA had the capacity to produce only about twenty studies each year, mandates removed a substantial portion of discretion over the agency's yearly agenda from board members, the director, and the committees.

OTA therefore tried to derail mandates before they became law, and often relied on board members to persuade their colleagues to remove the mandate language. When the Surface Transportation Act of 1987 was being deliberated in the Senate, language was added to the House version of the bill requiring OTA to conduct a massive study of the U.S. transportation infrastructure. As one OTA staffer put it, the study would have "broken the bank" at OTA because of the huge commitment of resources that would have been needed. OTA learned of the potential mandate late, as the conference on the bill was underway. But enough time was left for Rep. Dingell, a board member, to enter the conference proceedings in the Senate's Environment and Public Works Committee room and successfully insist that the language requiring the study be removed.

Another of the board's functions that distinguished OTA from some of the other support agencies was its responsibility for appointing the agency director. Whereas the head of GAO is appointed by the president, and the director of CRS by the Librarian of Congress, OTA's director was chosen by legislators on the board of directors. The choice of director was for many years especially sensitive because of controversy surrounding the first two people to hold the position. Directing OTA required a somewhat unusual mix of technical skills and political acumen, and because the agency did not make policy, the position of director offered little direct political power in return for its demands. The director's term was six years in length, although only one person, John Gibbons, served a complete term. OTA had four directors over the course of its history (not including three interim acting directors), and these are listed in Table 3.

STAFFING AND BUDGET

OTA's staff was never large. In 1995, its final year, 189 permanent employees worked at the agency, organized into six operating programs, each headed by a program director who reported to one of two assistant directors. The management structure was therefore sparse, with only two levels of hierarchy between analysts and the head of the agency. This lean structure won praise for its effectiveness and efficiency.[10] About 75 percent of the permanent staff at OTA were researchers. Dozens of temporary employees worked on various studies at OTA, and the agency further supplemented its staff with a large body of consultants and contractors, much as Rep. Mosher had insisted it should in 1972. In this way, it drew upon a much wider circle of expertise than could ever be available inside a single agency, especially one as small as OTA. Consultants came from industry and academia. For instance, in a 1991 study of manufacturing in the United States, entitled *Competing Economies: America, Europe, and the Pacific Rim*, OTA supplemented its own staff of nine analysts with an additional eight contractors. This report, like most from the agency, represented a broad range of exper-

Table 3. OTA DIRECTORS

Emilio O. Daddario	Nov. 1, 1973–Jul. 1, 1977
Daniel DeSimone (acting)	Jul. 1, 1977–Jan. 23, 1978
Russell Peterson	Jan. 23, 1978–Mar. 31, 1979
Daniel DeSimone (acting)	Mar. 31, 1979–Jun. 20, 1979
John H. Gibbons	Jun. 20, 1979–Jan. 28, 1993
Roger Herdman (acting)	Jan. 28, 1993–May 5, 1993
Roger Herdman	May 6, 1993–Sept. 30, 1995

tise that was evaluated, refined, and distilled by the agency into a useable form for Congress.

Like all congressional organizations, OTA received its funding through the legislative branch appropriations bill. Between 1980 and 1995, the agency's budget was nearly flat in real terms, at a level of roughly $22 million (1995 dollars), reflecting a remarkably long period without growth. The agency never engaged in a strategy of rapid expansion, and congressional appropriators just kept the agency's budget apace with inflation in most years. OTA's funding mechanism meant that committees that requested studies did not pay for them directly, an arrangement that occasionally brought criticism for encouraging overuse or inappropriate use of OTA and the other support agencies. Fiscal austerity in Congress began to squeeze the agency's budget in 1992, and its budget shrank a few percent each year through fiscal year 1995.

COMMITTEE CLIENTS AND THE DESIGN OF STUDIES

In the 1990s, OTA produced between twenty and thirty major reports annually, representing an average gross cost to Congress of a little less than $1 million per study. In 1995,[11] for instance, it released twenty-five major studies.

During the 1980s and 90s, the most regular committee clients for OTA were the House Commerce Committee, the House Science Committee, and the Senate Labor Committee. Typically, about one-quarter of the agency's studies were performed for committees chaired by one of its board members. After the early 1980s, most studies were sponsored by more than one committee. A 1987 report on Alzheimer's disease for instance, was requested jointly by Senate Finance, Senate Labor and Human Resources, Senate Special Committee on Aging, Senate Veterans Affairs, House Energy and Commerce, House Science, Space and Technology, and the House Select Committee on Aging. This multiple sponsorship meant that all seven committees had the opportunity to help frame the research questions and were given the opportunity to release the report at its conclusion, with whatever "spin" and credit-claiming they chose. Table 4 shows the committees most active in requesting OTA studies in the 1980s and 90s.[12]

OTA studies were initiated by a written request from a committee chair to the agency director or board. These letters of request were generally a few pages in length, stating the nature and importance of the issues at hand, and posing several specific questions to be answered. These requests typically followed a period of consultations between OTA employees and committee staff, who discussed the proposed study and came to an agree-

Table 4. TOP 10 COMMITTEE CLIENTS FOR OTA. WITH NUMBER OF
REQUESTS TO OTA, 1980–95

House Commerce	67
House Science	64
Senate Labor	54
Senate Commerce	45
Senate Government Affairs	37
Senate Foreign Relations	28
House International Relations	24
Senate Environment and Public Works	19
House Government Reform and Administration	19
Senate Energy	18

ment about its proposed parameters. OTA analysts often helped draft the language of the letters that formally requested studies. These consultations gave the agency an opportunity to shape the content of the requests it eventually received, and to head off written requests that the agency preferred not to accept. OTA staff also sometimes informally solicited requests for studies in their conversations with Hill staff, although this practice was officially frowned upon. Individual analysts sometimes went in search of projects, typically when a major study had concluded and the agency sought to maintain the expertise and resources it had developed for that study.

OTA studies typically required about two years for completion, during which time the agency often released a variety of interim reports or papers, as well as presenting testimony at hearings or in briefings. The length of time OTA dedicated to reports became a source of complaints by legislators and their staff. While not long in academic terms, two years can be long enough to diminish the political value of a study of a rapidly moving issue.

The agency spent a great deal of energy attempting to design studies that were readable and accessible to busy legislators and staff not inclined to spend time digesting lengthy tomes. Observers of OTA sometimes joked that the only legislator who ever read an entire OTA report was Albert Gore, Jr., jokingly called "Senator Science," and who, it was reported, could sometimes be seen with an OTA report on the floor of the Senate. For staff and legislators less committed than Al Gore, OTA provided one-page summaries of its studies, and often selected catchy names for reports that belied the academic nature of the contents. A 1989 report on urban air pollution from ozone, for example, had the jaunty title *Catching Our Breath.* An earlier study on alternative rockets for space launch vehicles was memorably called *Big Dumb Boosters.*

But to effectively catch the attention of staffers and legislators an advisory agency must do more than package its work palatably. Analysts at OTA knew that rarely will a legislator ever read a report, and that even among staff few will ever read a report in its entirety. As one agency analyst put it, "Members do not have time to read; staff have time to read but not to think; we are the ones with time to think."

One key to conveying the product of this "thinking" to an institution flooded with reports and studies of all kinds was the personal contacts that OTA analysts built with congressional staff. Just as personal relationships provide access for lobbyists attempting to make their cases on Capitol Hill, so did such contacts provide the basis for much dissemination of policy expertise from OTA to Congress. This style of communication meant that OTA was most successful when it could present its work to members and staff with a personal face. Congressional staff often pointed out that they relied on specific individuals at OTA whom they trusted, as well as on the reputation of the organization as a whole. Most staff whose committees used OTA studies claimed that personal contacts, telephone calls, meetings, and briefings were just as important if not more so than written reports.

Information is best conveyed from expert to politician in the context of relationships of familiarity and trust. Yet despite the importance of personal relationships, OTA did not represent to Congress only a collection of familiar experts. The institution itself had a character and significance that were crucial in determining its credibility. Congressional staff sometimes reported that while they almost never read very much of an OTA report, preferring to rely on what they learned from trusted individuals at the agency, it was essential to them that the thick volume with OTA's name on the spine be "sitting on the shelf" to back up what they were told by individuals. The legitimacy of the personal relationships that OTA analysts built on the Hill depended in large measure on the credibility of OTA as an institution. This tension, between the need for personal familiarity and for institutional neutrality and credibility, was one of the defining features of OTA as an organization.

THE POLITICAL UTILITY OF INFORMATION FROM OTA

A certain amount of mystery surrounded the use of OTA studies in Congress. Concrete indicators of the agency's influence on policy-making are difficult to identify—a problem not specific to OTA but one often encountered with policy experts of all kinds.

The patterns of influence that link knowledge and expertise to specific policy outcomes are often hidden at best, and impossible to trace at worst. Rarely would a responsible legislator cast a vote simply on the basis of an expert study or recommendation. The political calculus of policy-making is vastly more complex than that. This fact meant that when challenged by budget cutters to justify its existence in 1995, OTA and its allies faced obstacles in citing simple, obvious measures of its utility to Congress. Indeed, it is impossible to identify a single bill where an OTA study was clearly decisive to the outcome—as measured in votes. Neither agency personnel, congressional staff, nor legislators interviewed for this study could cite a single case where a member of Congress voted for or against a bill chiefly on the basis of an OTA study. The claims of experts such as OTA are just one ingredient in the mix of values and interests, partisanship, ideology, district concerns, loyalties and commitments, rivalries, and career aspirations that combine in every policy decision. Moreover, experts often do not present their ideas and assertions directly to legislators. Instead these reach members through staff, the media, and others.

For all these reasons, measuring the influence of OTA on Congress is not so simple as counting and characterizing votes somehow shaped by the agency. Anecdotal evidence suggests that OTA influenced the policy process in at least two main ways, rhetorically and analytically. Occasionally, the main value of an OTA study to legislators was its usefulness as a resource for persuading others or for justifying a policy position. For example, in April 1993, Representative Pete Stark introduced amendments to the Orphan Drug Act of 1983 aimed at regulating pricing practices in the pharmaceutical industry for drugs used to treat rare diseases. Stark charged pharmaceutical companies with egregious pricing practices for charging patients as much as $300,000 per year for drugs. To support his charges, Stark relied in a prominent way on two OTA studies which he summarized in his floor statement, claiming that OTA had documented "gross abuse" of patients by several firms.[13]

On occasion, legislators' rhetorical use of OTA studies was transparent. In August 1977, Texas Senator John Tower used studies from OTA and other congressional agencies to blast the Carter administration's energy policy, which he felt did not sufficiently emphasize "free-market operations" and increases in domestic oil production. On the floor of the Senate, Tower argued that the Carter plan had "glaring shortcomings," and that the expert studies proved his point.[14] Just a year later, Tower's colleague from Texas, Senator Lloyd Bentsen, couched his advocacy of the state's oil interests in the language of another OTA policy study. Bentsen had introduced a bill to decontrol the price of oil produced by high-risk "tertiary recovery" techniques, and he used OTA analysis to build a case in his floor statement.[15] No one believed that Tower and Bentsen had come to their views on the oil industry on the basis of OTA research. Rather, the research represented convenient ammunition to be used in support of existing preferences.[16]

In other cases, OTA's work played a role more consistent with rational models of politics, in which the utility of information derives from its capacity to reduce uncertainty.[17] For example, soon after OTA's creation in 1974, Secretary of Defense James Schlesinger requested congressional funding for Counterforce, a nuclear weapons targeting strategy. Under the Counterforce doctrine proposed by the Pentagon, the United States and U.S.S.R. would target only strategic sites, rather than population centers. The result was to be a reduction in casualties resulting from a nuclear exchange, to a fraction of the 100 million estimated for an all-out nuclear war, according to a Defense Department analysis.

The proposal presented a classic problem for legislators. The crux of the policy was a technical claim, namely that in a so-called Counterforce war, only 0.5 million to 6 million casualties would occur. One's position on the issue depended in a central way upon whether one believed the technical claim, but no legislator was in a position to conduct the original analysis necessary to verify that claim. The Pentagon had what was essentially a monopoly on information about the subject. Many legislators were uncertain about the figures and wanted verification. (Others, like Senator Edmund Muskie, worried that, accurate or inaccurate, talk of such relatively limited destruction in a war—compared to losses of half a nation's population—could increase the likelihood of a nuclear exchange.) In response to a desire for analysis of the Pentagon's claim, Senate Foreign Affairs Committee Chair John Sparkman requested that the new OTA undertake a technical review of the Counterforce concept. The agency complied, and in February 1975 released a report criticizing the DOD casualty estimates. OTA argued that the figures were overly optimistic, and on the basis of the review, Sparkman wrote to Schlesinger asking for revisions of the estimates using "more realistic" assumptions. In this instance, legislators sought the OTA research to shed light on a poorly understood problem, rather than to build a stronger case for existing policy preferences.

These two roles for policy expertise—rhetorical and analytic—were by far the most common and important uses for information from OTA. They represent modal forms of "knowledge utilization" in the policy process, and are the subject of a perennial debate about the politics of expertise. Is analysis adopted by political actors to support or rationalize existing preferences—as in the Texas senators' case?[18] Or does analysis and expertise shape policy by contributing to the formation of policy preferences on the part of those who use it—as in Sparkman's case?

The answer is, clearly, both, but in OTA's case something like the latter was more typical. Traces of legislators' use of OTA studies to rationalize policy positions are not common. To find evidence, one might ask how often legislators referred to OTA in their public statements about policy. As they explained their positions, justified and rationalized choices, tried to persuade others, or attempted to claim credit, to what extent did legislators appeal to OTA studies? It would be ideal to sample every policy speech by every legislator, made in Washington and around the country, and then conduct a content analysis to look for traces of OTA's influence. But that would be an obviously futile undertaking. Yet it is possible to examine legislators' statements in the *Congressional Record*. Statements there, whether actual utterances on the floor of the House or Senate, subsequent revisions to oral statements, or written insertions, provide a synopsis of legislators' rhetorical styles and substance that can be readily analyzed. Statements in the *Record* can be a useful window on the content of policy debates and rhetoric.

It is possible to identify every remark in the *Record* that refers directly to OTA. When one does so, an unmistakable finding stands out: the agency is nearly absent from twenty-three years' worth of political rhetoric in the *Record*. During the 1980s and 1990s, Congress's 535 legislators together referred to an OTA study by name less than once a month. Moreover, OTA citations in the *Record* actually *declined* annually in the 1980s and 1990s, despite the fact that the agency's annual output in studies doubled during this period. The more work OTA produced for legislators, the less they referred to it in their public statements. While legislators may occasionally use analysis and claims from OTA work without mentioning or even knowing its source, this evidence tends to confirm a common perception among observers of Congress that OTA did not contribute in a substantial way to policy rhetoric. It is little wonder that a San Diego newspaper article on OTA in 1991 ran under the title, "The Office of WHAT?"[19]

If, as most of the staff and agency analysts interviewed for this study believe, and *Congressional Record* data suggest, OTA's utility to Congress did not lie in its contributions to political discourse, then what role did the agency's studies play? The answer can be found by looking at the earliest stages of the legislative process, where policy proposals are formulated and the policy agenda set. Interviews with congressional staff reveal that OTA's main function in the legislature was to identify and frame issues, to help focus committees' and legislators' attention, and to help them develop and analyze policy alternatives. It turns out that by the time bills were formulated, debated, and voted upon—the activities typically best represented in the *Record*—OTA had almost always dropped away from the policy process.

The words of congressional staff themselves help explain this fact. A House staffer reports that OTA played the greatest role before a bill was drafted, saying that for using OTA analysis, "it's too late once you have a bill." The reason legislators and their staff went to OTA in the first place was that "you want to know, how big a problem is it—what are the consequences?" Another says the agency's expertise was helpful "when you start to get into an issue, in framing it and asking, 'is there a problem? What's the problem? Are we going in the right direction?'" Another staffer says that OTA was useful to committees "at the very beginning, before positions are arrived at." Others confirm that by the time legislators drafted a bill, the experts at OTA were "not part of the process," and "once positions are determined, it's too late [for experts to matter]."

A good illustration of this role for expertise in policy-making involves a bill marked up in a subcommittee of the Senate Committee on Governmental Affairs in 1980. The bill was intended to require chemical marking of commercial explosives during the manufacturing process, in order to aid law enforcement agencies in investigating bombings. OTA was asked to research the utility of such a program, which was strongly opposed by explosives manufacturers. When the agency described three alternatives for legislative action in its study, the subcommittee considering the bill structured its report around the agency alternatives, voting explicitly among "OTA Option 1," "OTA Option 2," and "OTA Option 3."

What is important about this case is that legislators in the subcommittee did not base their choices among options on the basis of the analysis, nor were votes on the floor decided on the basis of the study. OTA's role was to help define the nature of the problem, to provide technical legitimation for various responses to it. The agency contributed to the structure for choice, rather than to judgements about how to choose. This function, although rarely in such a bald form, was characteristic of the agency's participation in the policy process, and legislators' interests in controlling this function established the basic set of incentives to which the agency responded.

Chapter 4

Building OTA:
The Separation of Powers

When OTA was established by the Technology Assessment Act of 1972, it became only the third legislative support agency in Congress' history. For more than a century, Congress had no staff agencies assisting it, until the creation of the Legislative Reference Service in 1914. In 1945, Congress designated the General Accounting Office a legislative agency, and then, three decades later, created OTA. What motivated legislators to add OTA to its small collection of internal agencies?

A common answer to this question is that given by Rep. Emilio Daddario, OTA's sponsor in the House. He explains the creation of a congressional agency in terms of public policy needs. Daddario notes that legislators did not have sufficient training or background to fully understand many environmental, defense, aerospace, and other technical problems facing the nation, and created OTA to better inform policy.[1] His account is supported by Rep. George Brown, one of the agency's strongest patrons in the 1980s and 90s.[2] Both legislators portray the goal of OTA's creation as improving the content of public policy. Smith's history of U.S. science policy also endorses this explanation, attributing the creation of the agency to concern with the social control of technology. He writes that "the establishment of the OTA represented an attempt to control technological change . . . to balance positive and negative effects of introducing new technologies."[3]

A different explanation of the agency's origins has been suggested by John Gibbons, the agency's longest-serving director. Gibbons describes OTA's beginnings in terms of inter-branch rivalry between Congress and the

White House, attributing the establishment of the agency to a desire by legislators to gain greater control over the power to make policy. The legislators' goal, in this view, was to create a captive source of expertise—one that they could control. OTA was a response to "a threat to the balance of power," rather than simply a solution to public policy problems, says Gibbons,[4] and his account is consistent with scholarship on inter-branch politics that locates OTA's origins in the context of the congressional reforms of the 1970s.[5] Gibbons suggests that legislators wanted more than just access to information. They *had* access to policy expertise; what they wanted was better control over the production of information. They wanted information that they could trust, that was responsive to their institutional interests and not those of an executive department or agency. The words of many legislators tend to endorse Gibbons's view that they saw in the Daddario subcommittee's plans for a new agency not just a means to better policy, but also a lever that might help tilt the balance of power back toward Congress and away from the increasingly hostile administration. Speaking on the floor in favor of the OTA legislation at the time, Rep. Charles Mosher commented, "Let us face it, Mr. Chairman, we are constantly outmanned and outgunned by the expertise of the executive agencies."[6] Rep. Olin Teague complained that as the technical content of legislation increased during the 1950s and 60s, congressional committees "had to depend more and more on experts from the executive branch. . . ."[7]

Reflecting on these concerns later, Rep. John Wydler commented that "the only real technical witnesses we heard from [in congressional hearings] were administration witnesses whose bias was obvious." Wydler says, "everything they were telling us was why the administration's program was the right one, that decisions that had been made were correct and so on. This feeling was that what we needed was an independent group of scientific people in the Congress whom we could turn to as more or less our expert witnesses. . . . I really believe that was the motivating idea behind setting up the OTA."[8]

Which account of OTA's origins is correct—Daddario's good-policy account or Gibbons's institutional power account? The answer is that both are right, and each is dependent upon the other. The two roles—informing policy choices and serving Congress' institutional interests—were intertwined for OTA. Policy questions gave rise to Daddario's proposal in the first place, and that proposal then succeeded because it tapped into a major reservoir of demand for control over information, one that was much broader than the original concerns with the content of science and technology policy. Although conflict with the Nixon administration passed soon after OTA's establishment, the impetus for OTA to serve institutional interests as well as policy interests, to be an "expert witness" for the legislature, provided a significant undercurrent of demand for information from OTA throughout its life.

OTA AS EXPERT WITNESS FOR CONGRESS

Over the years, fulfilling the role of expert witness for Congress involved several kinds of activity not described in the language of the Technology Assessment Act prepared by Daddario's subcommittee. These included assisting with oversight, serving as a surrogate source of expertise for uncooperative agencies, and reducing legislators' uncertainty about the implications of major White House policy initiatives.

Assisting with congressional oversight was probably the furthest removed of OTA's activities from its statutory charter, but it became inseparable from the agency's formal mission. A wide range of committees used OTA to evaluate agency plans and activities. OTA performed critiques of a Federal Aviation Administration system plan, Veterans Administration mortality rate tabulations, and Post Office plans for automation. It provided general reviews of the Environmental Protection Agency, the 1976 Energy Research and Development Administration plan, and Energy Department conservation and solar energy programs and fusion energy activities.

It also conducted a review of the Social Security Administration's computer procurement strategy, for the House Appropriations Committee in 1993 and 1994. In that study, OTA was critical of the Social Security Administration's plans for using new computer equipment. As a result of the OTA study, the committee rescinded current year appropriations and then deferred over $360 million in future Social Security purchases until the Administration could convince legislators that the equipment would be well used. In this case, and in many others, legislators used OTA expertise both as a check on agency claims and as a surrogate for agency information where their relationships with agencies were not good, or where they found agency experts insufficiently forthcoming.

Having a source of independent information often proved useful where legislators were attempting to act aggressively in the face of agency reluctance to embrace new policies. During the 1980s, environmental legislation produced numerous opportunities for OTA to fill gaps in expertise left by agencies led by Reagan appointees averse to stronger environmental policies. Legislators turned to OTA for studies of radioactive and medical waste, the Montreal Protocol on ozone depletion, acid rain and clean air, groundwater, Superfund site cleanup, and offshore oil and gas development.

In the case of the monumental Clean Air Act Amendments of 1990, committees requested a sizeable commitment of help from OTA during the decade-long legislative cycle that produced the amendments. The agency issued two major reports on clean air during this time, *Acid Rain and Transported Pollutants* (1984), and *Catching Our Breath: Next Steps for Reducing Urban Ozone* (1989). It also provided several interim reports and a considerable number of consultations and briefings with staff and members. A Senate Environment Committee aide who was involved with the Clean Air Act Amendments says, "When the Reagan administration came in, we had less access to EPA, and we were concerned about [the validity of] the material we got. This was a major factor in our turning to OTA for analysis on clean air."

This staffer says that as a general matter, when seeking out expert advice her committee wants "someone who is disinterested from both the regulator standpoint and the regulated." In the case of asbestos, she remarked, "EPA is being sued over asbestos—you can't ask them [for analysis]." She also cited the case of congressional review of the effects of Agent Orange in Vietnam, saying, "OTA is filling an important role because they're not a federal agency that's involved."

A House Science subcommittee staff director comments that OTA's report on biological diversity was valuable because it identified gaps in federal agency activities, and "we wouldn't have gotten that from the executive branch." He says that OTA's work on Superfund and other environmental issues "identified shortcomings in implementation or the statutory base that the executive branch wouldn't point out."

OTA's utility as an independent expert witness for Congress was probably most evident in Congress' responses to major executive branch policy initiatives. When the White House announced major programs with technical content, or justified a policy proposal with expert claims, committees in Congress often turned to OTA for independent verification. It is interesting to note that this type of "expert witness" role occurred more often in some policy areas than in others. Congress' historical disadvantage in expert resources is substantially greater in defense and space than in areas such as health care or economic policy, where a greater supply of independent policy experts without ties to executive programs is available.[9]

Many of OTA's contributions to policy-making occurred in defense policy, where the executive branch enjoys a near-monopoly over policy information. The Carter administration's announcement of a basing plan for the MX missile in 1979 is a prime example. As had been the case with Schlesinger's Counterforce plan several years before, the proposal for basing two hundred nuclear missiles was fraught with uncertainty for many legislators. By the time of Carter's announcement of MX plans, a number of basing alternatives had been considered at the Pentagon. The goal was to allow U.S.

missiles to survive a pre-emptive attack in one or more ways: by hardening missile silos, by concealing missiles, by making launchers mobile, by deceiving the Soviets about U.S. missiles with electronic countermeasures, or by providing anti-missile defenses. Which of these options was best, and what means ought to be used to achieve it, was a matter of much disagreement among legislators and policy experts.

In August, the Carter administration announced that it had chosen a mobile basing system for MX known as the "racetrack," in which the two hundred missiles would be moved about a track among twenty-three hardened shelters. In Congress, legislators took a detailed interest in the specifics of the proposal. In a May 1980 request for a study of MX by OTA, Rep. Morris Udall and Sen. Ted Stevens wrote that Congress needed "the best obtainable information and analysis," and that there would be "particular value" in an assessment which was "independent of the Defense Department and the Administration."[10]

In its 1981 report, OTA presented analyses of five possible basing schemes for MX, all of which the agency judged to involve serious risks, uncertainties, and high costs. The information contained in the report strengthened legislators' hands in bargaining with the administration, and it added to a growing wave of public skepticism about the usefulness of the MX system.[11] It served as both a rhetorical tool for those predisposed against MX and an informative resource for those uncertain about how to proceed. In October 1981, the Reagan administration abandoned Carter's racetrack scheme in favor of placing just one hundred missiles temporarily in existing Minuteman and Titan II missile silos. In December, Congress further watered down the MX in a defense appropriations bill, limiting funds that could be used for development of "superhardened" silos.

Ronald Reagan's proposal for the Strategic Defense Initiative two years later placed Congress in a similar situation. SDI's viability turned on highly technical matters, as had MX and Counterforce. Congress used OTA to verify the administration's promise of a national "shield" against nuclear weapons. The agency released the first in a series of studies in 1984, taking an unusually pointed stance for OTA.[12] The study was prepared by Ashton Carter, who was working at the time as an independent contractor to OTA. Carter argued that the prospects of SDI's actually functioning as advertised by the administration were remote. Carter's criticisms, carrying OTA's imprimatur, caught the attention of the media and the major participants in the SDI debate. The report was unusual in the level of visibility it garnered and in the extent to which it was used as ammunition by opponents of the policy.

The Pentagon reacted forcefully to the challenge from the tiny congressional agency, criticizing OTA's technical claims and going so far as to formally request that the OTA director disavow the report. Instead of recanting, Gibbons convened a panel of reviewers to evaluate the paper. This group largely endorsed the findings, and OTA stood by its study, to the dismay of Pentagon officials unaccustomed to such a strident technical critique from Congress. The dispute between OTA and the Defense Department drew attention to the technical foundation of SDI. Questions about cost and strategy aside, OTA gave credence to the growing impression of many observers that the White House was exaggerating what was possible technically. Reagan appointees at the Pentagon became increasingly defensive about their plans for SDI, shifting from an offensive posture, in which they had been attempting to sell the program, to a defensive posture in which they devoted their resources to defending their own assertions. In this sense alone, the agency's study was an accomplishment from the congressional perspective, since not often can members of Congress place the Pentagon on a defensive footing over the technical aspects of a program. By no means was OTA the source of all technically based opposition, but its study brought uncertainties surrounding SDI more clearly into public view and contributed to a loss of political momentum for the program by 1986.

In 1987, OTA finished a comprehensive study initiated by opponents of SDI on the House Appropriations Committee. The agency provided classified and non-classified versions in October. The report criticized SDI on several fronts, questioning the feasibility of meeting program goals, predicting that the first phase of SDI deployment would not be ready until 1995–2000 at best, and that it would be able to destroy only a modest fraction of Soviet warheads. The study said that so much uncertainty surrounded later stages of SDI deployment that ten years would be required to even judge their feasibility.

This round from OTA drew another attack from the Pentagon, which denounced the report and tied up the public version by claiming that it revealed classified information.[13] After a series of negotiations, the report was finally released with modifications in May 1988. In the preface, the OTA authors charged "some in the Defense Department" with attempting to stifle public debate over the pros and cons of ballistic missile defense.[14]

By the time the classification struggle ended, the agency's criticisms of SDI had become well known in the defense community, and were contributing to an emergent view held by many that SDI was not viable except as a set of long-range research programs. OTA provided what one Senate staffer involved calls "key ammunition" for those attempting to build a case against SDI. By the late 1980s, OTA's critiques had become widely accepted as the standard wisdom about SDI for all but a few diehard advocates.

OTA's capacity to mitigate Congress's disadvantage in expert information in this way is also illustrated in the energy policy arena. During the 1970s, struggles to rationalize and improve the nation's energy policies presented circumstances similar to those of Counterforce, MX, and SDI in technical complexity and political uncertainty. Between 1974 and the end of the Carter administration in early 1981, OTA issued fifteen major reports and a handful of memoranda and background papers on energy issues. This body of work represented more than one-fifth of the agency's total output of studies for the period 1974–1980.[15]

The most notable case involved President Carter's first National Energy Plan. The administration abruptly announced the immense plan in April 1977, taking members of Congress and the energy establishment somewhat by surprise, despite the fact that Carter had promised to produce a plan within ninety days of taking office. Energy planning had proven a lingering morass for both of Carter's predecessors, and the group that had drafted the plan under the direction of James Schlesinger had been highly secretive about its progress. In meeting the ninety-day presidential deadline, the group failed to consult with important energy policy-makers, including key committee chairs on the Hill.[16] The group's plan was a massive, complex package of legislation that touched on nearly every technical uncertainty and every political interest in the energy arena.

The complexity, size, and secrecy of the energy plan overwhelmed many legislators, and stirred a hornets' nest of opposition from nearly every group with an interest in energy. As members scrutinized the proposals, it became clear that Schlesinger's group had been hasty with its technical analysis and estimates. Questions arose as to whether the plan's projections and assumptions could be substantiated.

A clumsy lobbying effort by the White House did not remedy the situation. The administration mishandled technical questions, prompting complaints by legislators that Congress was receiving insufficient and even incorrect information.[17] To help reduce some of the uncertainties associated with the plan, legislators requested reviews from all four congressional support agencies—an unusually pointed effort to bring expert resources within Congress to bear on White House policy.

OTA's study, completed in just four months, was critical of the plan, stating that its proposed actions were not strong enough to solve the oil import problem, and that its objectives for domestic energy production would not likely be met. These criticisms were consistent with the findings of the other congressional support agencies. The combined reports represented a solid technical indictment of the energy plan and worked to undermine the plan's already shaky political prospects.[18]

In this case, as in others, what was notable about OTA was not that the agency instructed legislators how to vote, but that it helped them establish a basis for their positions. OTA's involvement in these debates over MX, SDI, and the 1975 Energy Plan illustrates an important point about the purposes of the agency: the policy goal of improving the intelligence of legislation can be difficult to separate from the institutional goal of maintaining independence from the executive. The dynamics of each are intertwined, and OTA served both goals at once. OTA's function was as much to increase legislators' authority with respect to the executive as to change the substance of policy.

In this regard, the congressional setting differs from that in governments with a parliamentary structure, where the impetus for legislative independence is not nearly as strong. It is worthwhile to pause from considering OTA to briefly compare its functions to those of analogous parliamentary agencies.

POLICY EXPERTS IN PARLIAMENTARY GOVERNMENT

The deliberations in the United States during the 1960s over the need for OTA, and the subsequent passage of the Technology Assessment Act in 1972, spawned a "technology assessment" movement in Europe in the 1970s that continued into the 1990s. There have been efforts in Germany, Great Britain, France, the Netherlands, and elsewhere to establish similar organizations. Many of these efforts have explicitly attempted to replicate OTA, or to adapt it to European systems. Many delegations from Europe visited OTA's office on Pennsylvania Avenue in an attempt to find the key to recreating its success.

The outcome of these efforts is foreshadowed by the fact that many European advocates of OTA-like organizations describe the utility of expert information in just the restricted terms Emilio Daddario used in the United States. They observe the pervasiveness of technology and its diverse social implications, expressing the same concern with forecasting positive and negative effects of innovation that framed some of the early OTA debate more than two decades ago.[19] The case for bringing scientists and engineers into the legislative process is made on the basis of the demands of contemporary policy problems.

But the other half of the formula is missing. Without the institutional mandate of serving an independent legislature, attempts to build European versions of OTA have met with slight success. Majority parties and governing coalitions have typically been content to leave expert analysis of policy to ministries, and have feared that agencies like OTA would increase the capacity of backbenchers or the opposition to weaken the government. In France, the Netherlands, Germany, the United Kingdom, and Denmark, governments have consistently resisted the creation of independent sources of expertise modelled on OTA.[20] While competing institutional interests do exist in European systems, institutional structures have not provided a natural or stable home for expert agencies modeled on OTA, and party politics has worked to circumscribe organizations that do emerge.

During an initial phase of interest in the 1970s, no attempts at institution-building succeeded, despite a number of concrete proposals.[21] A second period of interest in "technology assessment," beginning in the mid 1980s, produced organizations in several nations, but none on even the modest scale of OTA or similar in technical capacity, political standing, or level of institutionalization. All have staffs of a couple dozen or fewer, for instance, and many have somewhat ambiguous charters and institutional loyalties.

In France, for example, efforts dating to 1976 to create a parliamentary agency were blocked for years by conservative governments. Proponents finally succeeded in 1983, in the climate of support for the constitutional strengthening of parliament created by the Mitterrand government. But the organization, called the *Office Parlementaire d'Évaluation des Choix Scientifique et Technologiques*, exists only as a parliamentary committee with a staff of a few people. Its capacities do not compare with those of OTA even a few years after its own founding.

The Netherlands experience was similar. The Netherlands Organization for Technology Assessment, created in 1986, originated in a four-year old ministry office. Despite being designated a parliamentary organization, the small staff of the office remains tied to the government's Minister of Education and Science.

Germany's *Büro für Technikfolgen-Abschätzung des deutschen Bundestages*, created only recently after nearly two decades of wrangling, has a tenuous status and institutional loyalties that are divided between a parliamentary committee on research and technology and the external Karlsruhe Nuclear Research Facility. The original proposal for a German office came from opposition parties in 1973, the year after OTA was established. This proposal, and numerous subsequent formulations, were resisted because there was little enthusiasm for strengthening the Bundestag as an institution.[22] In the debate on the *Büro*, some opponents who recognized the differences between Congress and the Bundestag in fact argued that the U.S. OTA could not be transferred to the German parliamentary system.[23]

In Britain, efforts to create a Westminster version of OTA by MPs in the mid-1980s were sidetracked by the Thatcher government, which refused to fund a parliamentary office. A compromise was reached and given the misleading name "Parliamentary Office of Science and Technology." The small organization is independent of the legislature and government.[24]

It is likely that these small European agencies will establish themselves further as years pass, but none appears positioned to develop into an institution with the national credibility that OTA had in the U.S. In the British, Dutch, and German cases, the agencies are not strictly servants of their respective parliaments, and none has a natural legislative clientele, as OTA did in the congressional committee system.

These European experiences reinforce the idea that Daddario's vision of OTA might have been a necessary ingredient in building OTA, but was not sufficient. The other ingredient was what Mosher called OTA's function as an expert witness for Congress.

This role as expert witness anticipates an interesting question. OTA Director John Gibbons has noted that OTA spent a great deal of energy in the 1980s "countering executive branch activism."[25] And during most of the 1970s, 1980s, and 1990s, OTA served a Democrat-controlled Congress while Republicans dominated the White House. It would seem reasonable to expect that OTA would have developed partisan loyalties that reflected the traditional pattern of divided control during this period. In fact, it is possible that what appears to be an institutional impetus for OTA was actually partisan; it was not so much Congress that wanted expertise independent of the executive, as it was Democrats who wanted leverage against Republican White Houses. Did OTA serve as a tool of Democratic legislators against Republican Presidents?

For a hint at the answer, one can examine evidence from OTA's records on the flow of requests from the House and Senate across periods of differing partisan configurations (i.e., purely divided control under Nixon, Ford, two years of Reagan, and Bush; unified control under Carter and two years of Clinton; and mixed control for Reagan's first six years).[26] But examination of these records does not reveal any pattern of elevated OTA activity prompted by Democratic committee chairs during Republican administrations. There was no clear connection between partisanship and the level of requests for assistance by OTA from the committees. If this rough indicator is correct, then somehow OTA became, in John Gibbons's words, "Congress' own little band," helping keep administration claims "honest" without obviously becoming partisan in the process.[27] The trick of separating institutional loyalty from partisan loyalty was a cornerstone of OTA's success; the next chapter looks at the evolution of the agency's ability to accomplish this task.

Chapter 5

Saving OTA: Party Politics and the Strategy of Neutrality

When legislators established OTA, many inside and outside Congress hoped that the new agency would provide the kind of objective advice that is a common mission of new expert organizations. The law indicated that one of OTA's main purposes was to equip Congress with the means for obtaining "competent, unbiased information."[1] Harvey Brooks, who chaired the 1968 study by the National Academy of Sciences that had encouraged the creation of an office like OTA, and who had then authored much of the bill, has commented that OTA was "designed to emphasize both the appearance and reality of non-partisan, neutral competence"—language that might have been taken directly from a Progressive era text on public administration.[2]

This idealized image of neutral expertise was hardly fulfilled in the agency's first years. After the passage of the law, the most important question surrounding the new agency was whether it would survive to establish itself as a player in policy-making, be dismissed as irrelevant, or even be abolished as a casualty of party politics.

In 1973, just months after Elford Cederberg's appropriations skirmish with Edward Kennedy, and even before OTA had begun its operations, partisan lines rapidly formed around OTA. Vocal new critics joined Cederberg in assailing the agency. They expanded on his argument, claiming that the new agency would end up serving as a tool for Senator Kennedy and other Democrats to use against the Nixon administration. In *The Wall Street Journal,* columnist Jude Wannisky charged that Kennedy had set OTA up as a "shadow government" for himself.[3] *The National Review* ran an article entitled "Teddy at Work," citing concern in the administration that Kennedy would shape OTA into a "political weapon" to be used against the administration.[4]

As 1974 arrived and OTA opened for business, its nascent reputation worsened. Attacks on the agency continued, and within five years it became clear that the agency's survival was in jeopardy. It was rent internally by divisions on its board of directors, and it had suffered a barrage of external criticism in the press from conservative critics such as William Safire. In fact, by the end of the 1970s, OTA appeared to be an utter failure at providing neutral expertise, having experienced an accelerated development from the goal of objectivity to the reality of politicization.

But consider the situation ten years later: a healthy and vigorous OTA was being praised in the press and around Capitol Hill for providing neutral and non-partisan policy advice to Congress. The agency could count among its friends Republicans such as Ted Stevens and Orrin Hatch. In a story carried by the Associated Press near the end of the decade, OTA received credit for being a "dispassionate, nonpartisan player."[5] The agency was cited for having earned "widespread trust" on Capitol Hill.[6]

Between 1980 and 1990, OTA underwent a dramatic change in fortune. Indeed, it evolved along a trajectory opposite to that predicted by the standard account of expert politicization, evolving from a high to a low degree of politicization. What accounts for this dramatic departure from the expected pattern of politicization?

The answer is not simply improved professional standards, a charismatic leader committed to balance, or the hiring of personnel that better adhered to the goal of scientific "objectivity"—although all these ingredients were present in varying degrees. The key to OTA's changed stature was its need to build and maintain for itself an internal clientele. Like most agencies, OTA's strength was a function of the strength of its constituency and the energy of its enemies. It did not take long for the agency to learn that to avoid controversy, protect its budget, and earn a measure of control over its internal affairs, it had to build for itself a supportive constituency within the legislature while converting as many of its enemies as it could. Though a mix of trial-and-error and calculation, OTA developed a *strategy of neutrality*. This strategy embraced the neutral competence ideal not as a professional standard but as a political survival strategy to ward off critics like Cederberg and Safire. The strategy evolved in two steps, first as a response to party politics, and then, after the early 1980s, as response to the centrifugal pull of the congressional committee system.

The development of the strategy provides an interesting illustration of organizational learning by OTA. The process involved adapting to an environment where power was shared, although not equally, between legislators of both parties. The origins of the strategy are to be found in the frustrations of some agency personnel and its congressional allies with the barrage of criticism of the mid- and late 1970s.

The charges by conservatives were by no means unfounded. The first board was named by the House and Senate leaderships on October 17, 1972, and consisted of Edward Kennedy, Ernest Hollings, Hubert Humphrey, Gordon Allott, Richard Schweiker, and Peter Dominick from the Senate, and Charles Mosher, John Davis, Earle Cabell, James Harvey, and Mike McCormack from the House.[7] Kennedy wanted the position of board chair, although the authorizing legislation specified that in even-numbered Congresses—the 92nd was in session—the position of chair was to go to a House member. So Kennedy's office stalled the first meeting through the end of the year. When the board met for the first time, the 93rd Congress was in session, qualifying Kennedy for the position. With some maneuvering to ensure that he was the most senior Democrat nominated to the board by Majority Leader Mike Mansfield, the group indeed chose him chair.

Kennedy convened the first meeting of the OTA Board on April 10, 1973, and was in a position to put his stamp on the new office. Ellis Mottur, an aide, drafted rules of procedure for OTA and Kennedy introduced them at the first board meeting. Kennedy and Mottur also laid the groundwork for the November selection of Democrat and ex-Member Emilio Daddario as the agency's first director.

These initial steps were fodder for the kinds of attacks levied in the press about OTA serving as a weapon against the Nixon administration, and they seemed to suggest that OTA would adopt anti-technology or anti-growth positions. While in Congress, Daddario had voted against the ABM missile defense system and the SST, prominent technology projects favored by the Nixon administration.

When OTA finally began operations in January 1974, problems with the agency's image worsened. Several board members proposed policy problems for study by OTA, and these requests formed the agency's initial research agenda. Senator Hollings of South Carolina, chair of the National Ocean Policy Study in the Senate, was interested in marine issues, and, in January 1974, requested a study of an international fishing limit in coastal waters. OTA complied, not just releasing a report for Hollings, but also establishing an "Oceans" program within the agency that went on to produce five major reports in its first three years.

Senator Hubert Humphrey urged OTA to focus on agriculture and food resources, issues of interest to the state of Minnesota. In response, the agency set up a "Food" program that released its first report in February

1976. Representatives Olin Teague and Charles Mosher joined in the rush to extract studies from OTA, proposing a study of materials resources, and, with Hollings, the study of Carter's national energy plan. Kennedy, who was chairing the Health subcommittee of Labor and Public Welfare, proposed a study of drug safety and efficacy.

In these initial thirty-six months, OTA had developed into an extended staff office for a small cadre of legislators, most of whom tended toward liberal politics. Its twelve board members treated the agency as if it were the staff of a joint committee, and OTA's agenda became that of its most interested board patrons.

Daddario's style as director contributed to the agency's tendency to cater to the particularistic interests of Board members. As a recent ex-Member, Daddario had a collegial relationship with the board, especially those members from the House. In the opinion of a number of OTA employees and Hill staff, Daddario was more attuned to meeting the political demands of the board than to establishing an environment of political independence for OTA.[8] With the larger congressional membership unfamiliar with the new OTA, and a handful of interested members paying close attention, Daddario's tactics were natural. One OTA employee recalls that Daddario's chief demand on him and others as analysts at OTA was to keep the board members happy and "out of his hair." To the agency's critics like Cederberg, this relationship between OTA and its legislator-board of directors seemed the fulfillment of their predictions: OTA had been captured by Kennedy, Humphrey, and other liberals.

The influence of OTA's small group of patrons was institutionalized in several ways, most importantly through a mechanism known as "Rule 12." The twelfth of the agency's brief list of rules drafted in Kennedy's office gave control over the agency's staff to board members. The rule gave the board authority to veto hiring decisions by the agency director, and most importantly, stipulated that the director was to appoint staff designated by the board chair and vice-chair, the two ranking members of the other party from the chair and vice-chair, and "such other personnel as the Board may deem necessary."[9]

The effect was that legislators on the board were able to place their own staff at the agency. Hubert Humphrey appointed an aide named J.B. Cordaro, who then directed the food information systems study the Senator had requested. Ted Stevens's staffer, William Davis, worked on projects relevant to interests in the Senator's state of Alaska.

It was clear to those inside and outside OTA that the agency's personnel practices provided potential for politicization of studies. In a discussion of Rule 12 at a board meeting the first year, Morris Udall and Charles Mosher expressed reservations about the practice of political appointments and urged "restraint" on their colleagues because of the impression they felt the appointments would give. Nonetheless, the majority of board members supported the practice. Senator Kennedy stated that he felt that any "special responsibilities" staff might have to individual Board members "would not be inconsistent with their principal role" as OTA employees.[10] Senator Humphrey indicated that he was willing to allow his staffer to "have responsibilities under Director Daddario with the understanding that he would be available [to me] whenever he is needed."

Perceptions of politicization at OTA persisted, undermining the agency's poor reputation among conservatives as well as liberals not on the agency's board. In 1976, Representative Olin Teague, chair of OTA's board for the 94th Congress, conducted a state-of-the-agency assessment, which he reported to the board and director in December. Teague criticized staff hiring practices and Rule 12, saying that "some staff and consultants are recruited on the basis of paper or political qualifications." Teague claimed that he could think of no reasonable rationale for involving the board in personnel matters. He called for the elimination of Rule 12, arguing that the rule was inequitable, obsolete, and dangerous."[11]

The OTA employee who by far drew the most political criticism was Kennedy's aide Mottur. Mottur served as Assistant Director of the agency, and wielded disproportionate influence. His connections with the Kennedy family went back to his work on John Kennedy's 1960 campaign, and he had an impressive set of political skills to show for his experience. Mottur's allegiance to Senator Kennedy made him the target of the Senator's critics from both sides of the aisle. Conservatives especially disliked the Kennedy-Mottur combination at OTA. Criticisms of the two broke into the open in May 1977, six months after Teague's report criticizing OTA staffing, when Emilio Daddario announced his surprise resignation as director of the agency. Daddario offered no credible public explanation for his departure, and the abrupt nature of the resignation sparked charges of political manipulation behind the scenes at OTA.[12] What might have remained a limited controversy for the agency developed into a larger crisis when Representative Marjory Holt, a conservative Republican serving as vice-chair of OTA's board, announced her resignation from the board a week later. Holt claimed that she could no longer function on the board because of Kennedy's control over the agency. Holt charged that Kennedy had taken over OTA for his own personal purposes, saying "Kennedy dominates the entire thing."[13] She claimed that Kennedy had forced Daddario's resignation so that Mottur could take over the position of director.

The press reported similar criticisms by Olin Teague, saying he was also considering resigning from the OTA board because of Kennedy's use of the agency "for his personal political purposes."[14] The most strident of the criticisms of OTA and Kennedy found a voice in an essay by William Safire in *The New York Times*, entitled, "The Charles River Gang Returns." Safire claimed that Kennedy had "begun a campaign for a far more impressive role in the play of American power," using OTA as "his vehicle." Safire's rhetoric was unrestrained: "[W]e can expect a flow of reports from the politicized Office of Technology Assessment in the future that show how right Senator Kennedy is on everything from medical research to mass transit, with the scientific community's seal of approval on everything that puts consumerism over the fight against inflation, environmentalism over capitalism." OTA had become a "happy hunting ground of Kennedy apparatchiks" and "liberal technocrats." [15]

Kennedy and Mottur denied these charges, but their denials were of little avail. It was clear in Kennedy's office that OTA's lack of credibility was undermining both its ability to contribute to the policy-making process and its utility to the Senator.[16] The search for a new director to replace Daddario provided Kennedy what appeared to be an opportunity to win back some conservative support for the agency. Mottur, who assisted Kennedy in conducting the search, removed his own name from consideration, a move aimed at responding to Holt's charges and what he called the "erroneous *perception* of partisanship that . . . filled the press in recent weeks through rumors, innuendos, and inaccuracy [emphasis in the original]."[17] Kennedy's plan was to find a sympathetic Republican to take the job, since a Republican director could improve the appearance of bipartisanship at OTA.

Kennedy's choice, which the board approved in a 7–5 vote on October 22, 1977, was Russell Peterson, ex-Governor of Delaware. Peterson seemed to fit Kennedy's bill. As a Ph.D. physical chemist with a career at DuPont, Peterson had scientific credibility. And he had the right party credentials as well, having served as a Republican governor and as Richard Nixon's Director of the Council on Environmental Quality.

But in policy outlook Peterson was more Democrat than Republican. From the small liberal wing of the party, he was an environmentalist given to the use of the word "holistic"; in 1980, he would endorse Carter. From the perspective of Kennedy and his allies, Peterson was just the medicine OTA needed.

From Peterson's own perspective, what OTA needed was greater independence from its board, not posturing toward the right. While not unsympathetic to Kennedy's positions on many policy issues, he did not want to head an organization beholden to a handful of legislators. He accepted the directorship with his eyes open about OTA's problems, and arrived at the agency in 1980 with a mission: reform of political influence.

He brought a strategy to OTA that was quite the opposite of his predecessor's. Whereas Daddario had been highly solicitous of legislators' personal interests, Peterson aimed to build a layer of insulation between the agency and its patrons in Congress. His first move was an initiative to take control of the agency's staff from board members by eliminating Rule 12. His proposal that the rule be abandoned and control over staff be given wholly to the director attracted the support of ten of the twelve board members, including Kennedy. The benefits of improving the credibility of the agency were clear; its reports would bear more weight if the agency was seen as less beholden to a few legislators, and board members could spend less time involved in squabbles over the agency's affairs.

Only two board members resisted the change, Senators Hollings and Stevens—one Democrat and one Republican. Peterson met their threats to resign from the board and cut the agency's appropriation by threatening to resign himself. In the face of his firmness and the support of the rest of the board, Hollings and Stevens backed down and acquiesced in Peterson's move.

Other components of his strategy included adding a new level of managerial control over staff, which precipitated Mottur's departure. He also mounted a massive survey-based effort to construct a research agenda independent of board members' interests. OTA surveyed several thousand people outside Capitol Hill about what the agency's research priorities should be, with the intent of producing a prioritized list of national policy problems based on expert opinion around the country. The exercise was a classic policy analyst's attempt at determining national priorities through technical, non-political means. It outraged many legislators who recognized it as a rejection of Congress's own agenda-setting processes. The findings were scrapped in the end, and Peterson earned a good deal of ill will on the Hill.

Clearly, OTA's direction had been shifted, but not necessarily in a direction legislators liked. The cost of change was high at OTA, and Peterson's style alienated many members. Some legislators who lost influence over OTA, like Hollings and Stevens, were more vociferous than the many other legislators who were gaining influence. Peterson found himself accused of minor improprieties in decorating his office, as some of his detractors looked for ways to apply pressure. His tenure grew increasingly rocky as he struggled to distance the agency from board members' parochial interests while also attempting to remain relevant. When he was offered the directorship of the Audubon Society, a position in which he had long been interested, Peterson jumped at the chance to leave the agency.

His sixteen months at OTA took the agency further into controversy, but had at the same time sown seeds of permanent change. Peterson had largely broken staff ties to members of Congress, Kennedy's influence was diminished and that source of criticism laid to rest, and a more non-partisan style of interaction was in place. The agency lacked a supportive clientele, but it was much less vulnerable to charges by conservatives that it served as a tool of liberals.

The board's search for a successor to Peterson reflected an emerging consensus among legislators that OTA needed to redouble its efforts at gaining credibility and ending conflict over its activities. The board chose John Gibbons, a physicist from Oak Ridge National Laboratory, whose style was a mix of those of Daddario and Peterson. Like Daddario, the new director proved very attentive to legislators' political needs, but like Peterson he insisted upon intellectual independence. Unlike nearly everyone previously associated with the agency, Gibbons's party affiliation was publicly unknown. By the time of Gibbons's appointment, it had become increasingly clear to board members that an agency managed by twelve members evenly divided between party and chamber would have to support a balance among their own interests to stabilize itself. When members asked Gibbons what he would do if he "found politics being played at the agency," Gibbons responded with the right answer for a board tired of infighting: "I would fire the person."[18]

Gibbons introduced his own strategy for interacting with Congress: establishing a culture of political neutrality, and combining it with a diplomatic attentiveness to legislators' often divergent individual needs. His aim was to neither play favorites, as OTA had done under Daddario, nor step back from legislators' political demands, as it had attempted under Peterson. His goal was balanced solicitousness of legislators' needs.

The new strategy was needed. By the time Gibbons was sworn in as director during June 1979—quoting the poetry of Edna St. Vincent Millay— the agency's survival was indeed in question. Many critics and supporters had already judged OTA a failure. After five years, it had been unable to earn a base of trust among more than a few legislators, and many thought the reforms instituted by Peterson had come too late. Rep. John Dingell commented to Gibbons when he began, "You're the last chance for OTA."[19]

Gibbons put his strategy to work immediately. In what he called the "Fourth of July Massacre," he fired about fifteen percent of his staff, including what he called "favorite sons" of board members—staff who had severed their official ties to the legislators but who maintained loyalties. In an attempt to give the agency a "careful focus on the clients"—regardless of party—he formalized a practice of sharing with Republican legislators requests for studies issued by Democratic committee chairs. This gave ranking minority members notice of the agency's work, as well as an opportunity to modify or amend their counterparts' requests. This practice stretched but did not violate OTA's authorizing legislation, which directed the agency to perform work at the request of committee chairs. The tactic gave Republicans a sense that OTA would look out for their interests as well as those of Democrats.

Gibbons's strategy of neutrality bore fruit almost immediately. Within a year of his arrival, OTA's prospects began to improve noticeably. Criticisms of the agency dropped off, and an increasing number of legislators began to take seriously the little agency's studies.

The reversal in the agency's reputation began none too soon, because the outcome of the 1980 election in the Senate presented OTA with a new set of committee bosses. Republican control of the chamber changed the landscape for OTA. The new Senate Majority Whip, Ted Stevens of Alaska, was also chair of OTA's board, and so the agency's ability to serve Republicans as well as Democrats was put to the test. The election produced consternation among some agency employees who knew Stevens as a "naysayer" on the board in previous years, and feared what might happen to the agency with Republicans controlling one chamber, given the recent history of Republican hostility.

Bigger problems for OTA lay in the change in control over two key subcommittees. The election brought to Washington Senator Mack Mattingly of Georgia, a new conservative with an anti-government agenda. Mattingly chose OTA as a target for trimming "excess" government spending, and he received two subcommittee chairs in the Senate that put him in a position to pursue this goal: the Legislative Branch subcommittee of Appropriations, and the Congressional Operations and Oversight subcommittee of Governmental Affairs. Mattingly let it be known that he viewed OTA as superfluous, and that he sought to "zero" its appropriation. It would be a small victory for the freshman attempting to make his mark in Washington.

Mattingly did his best to mount a campaign against OTA, claiming that Congress needed "action rather than research." He did not attract much support for his cause from other Republicans, but benefitted from attention given to Donald Lambro's book *Fat City*, a 1980 hit list of "superfluous" and "wasteful" government agencies—among them OTA—which the Reagan administration was endorsing.

Mattingly's attack brought a response that surprised many. Led by Stevens, board members—including Republicans—rallied to the agency, in part miffed by the presumptions of the freshman who was venturing onto their turf. Stevens noted to board members in April that the effort to abolish OTA was "on our side," and Rep. George Brown lamented the persistence of the false impression that "Ted [Kennedy] is still chairman and Daddario still the executive director."[20]

Stevens developed a two-pronged strategy for defending OTA. First, he solicited letters of support for OTA from friends in Congress and from the new Republican committee chairs. Then he led a fight in the Appropriations subcommittee. Stevens and other board members Hatfield and Hollings sat on Mattingly's subcommittee, and together the three sustained OTA's budget at about two-thirds of its request. In the full committee and then on the floor, the three prevailed, restoring most of the funds cut by Mattingly.

Having lost the appropriations fight, Mattingly tried again a year later, this time through his Governmental Affairs subcommittee, scheduling an oversight hearing with the aim of deauthorizing the agency. This time Republican Senator Mathias rose to lead the agency's defense. Mathias preempted Mattingly's hearing with his own oversight hearing in the Rules Committee, where he called a list of favorable witnesses to praise the agency's accomplishments. With the Mathias hearings on record, Mattingly dropped his plans for a less accommodating event, and abandoned his efforts to take on OTA and its new Republican friends.

The "Mattingly affair," as some OTA staff called it, emerged as a turning point in OTA's history, as well as presaging the disaster it would encounter in one of the same subcommittees fourteen years later. The lone-wolf effort by Mattingly had rallied other Republicans with a new sense of propriety about OTA, and had resulted in ringing endorsements by key members of the party—something that would have been unimaginable in Daddario's or Peterson's tenure. Gibbons had indeed arrived in the nick of time, and had hit on a strategy for providing expertise to Congress that seemed successful.

The agency's struggles between 1974 and the early 1980s offered several interesting lessons for OTA about legislators' demands for information, and they were lessons that were not lost on the agency. From the beginning, legislators had insisted that the agency accept their own agenda. Not only Kennedy, but Hollings, Humphrey, Teague, Mosher, and others had demanded that OTA direct itself to policy problems of special interest to them. So OTA was not to be an independent think tank, merely funded by Congress, but would be a support agency for legislative issues.

More significantly, legislators had shown themselves to be intensely interested in how OTA's activities affected the balance of power in Congress. The Mattingly affair notwithstanding, most seemed more acutely aware of whether OTA's expertise advantaged their rivals than whether it improved the content of public policy. By 1981, staff at OTA had learned a lesson that had gone unnoticed in the first half-dozen years or so. Where a policy study appeared to favor one interest over another, the agency could count on those who felt slighted to be much more vociferous than those who were favored. Legislators with reason to object to an OTA study could make trouble for the agency that far outweighed whatever accolades might come from those whose position the agency might have supported. Favoritism did not seem to pay; a better approach was to offer something for everyone.

Chapter 6

Sustaining OTA: Committee Politics and the Strategy of Neutrality

The new strategy for sustaining OTA was proving its worth by late 1981 and early 1982. Assiduous attention to the interests of both parties minimized complaints about the agency's work. When it released neutrally framed studies designed to offer something for everyone, OTA found that no one would step forward to attack the agency for *not favoring* his or her interests. But it could count on quite the opposite happening when studies were obviously supportive of a particular policy position. And in an institution as decentralized as Congress, almost any enemy could turn out to be a dangerous one.

One measure of the agency's new success was a growing clientele and increasing interest from committees that had not solicited studies in the agency's early days. In 1982, the agency received requests for studies from twenty committees, almost a doubling of its base of clients from the mid-1970s. It was still not a widely known institution among the full membership, but it had established for itself a satisfactory reputation among those who counted most: Republican committee chairs in the Senate and Democratic chairs in the House.

With the expansion in OTA's market for studies came a new kind of problem: tussles among committees over the agency's work. With many committees now soliciting studies, opportunities arose for conflict among competing jurisdictions. The problem was virtually a recapitulation of what OTA had been through with Democrats and Republicans, this time with turf rather than party as the rub. Committee chairs were accusing one another of undue influence over the agency's work, fearing that studies would be framed and reported in such as way as to favor one jurisdictional interest over another.

With the partisanship question largely laid to rest, this new issue grew to be the major strategic challenge in sustaining a good relationship with Congress in the 1980s. The issue was another dimension of the same problem it had struggled with since Russell Peterson had arrived: successfully serving as an agent to multiple principals. OTA was confronting the fact of congressional decentralization and fragmentation of power. To serve as a expert advisor to the modern Congress meant doing something very different than the President's expert advisors were doing, namely simultaneously advising a host of competing interests, whether in the two parties or on the many committees. OTA did not take long to learn that Democrats on one committee could be just as jealous of the agency's work for Democrats on another as Republicans could be of its work for Democrats more generally.

Just the initiation of a study at OTA could signal among committees about their policy intentions, and often precipitated maneuvers for influence over the production of the report. In July 1987, for instance, the Senate Energy Committee requested a study from OTA on the development of natural resources—oil—in the Alaska National Wildlife Refuge (ANWR). The committee had begun a set of hearings on ANWR, and was faced with what Committee Chair Bennett Johnston called "differences in the perceived importance attached to the area's wilderness, wildlife and mineral resources." Wrapped up in these differences were technical disagreements about the nature of the physical impacts of alternative development proposals. In a letter to OTA, Johnston asked the agency to study the "environmental and economic impacts of oil development on the North Slope," and the "relevance of these impacts to ANWR." Johnston directed OTA to take into account the "potential evolution of oilfield development technology and practices over time."[1] Behind Johnston's request was the hope that OTA would argue that experience with oil production at Prudhoe Bay in Alaska, combined with recent technological developments, lessened environmental objections to development in ANWR.

Three days after Johnston's letter, Rep. Walter Jones, Chair of the House Merchant Marine Committee, wrote to OTA in an angry tone stating that he was "disturbed to learn in the eleventh hour" of the Senate request. Jones stated, "The Committee on Merchant Marine and Fisheries, which I chair, has jurisdiction over activities within the units of the National Wildlife Refuge System," and asserted that his committee would also be a sponsor of the study. Jones directed OTA not to pursue the study "without further modification and input from my staff."[2]

Referring to the conflict at a board meeting, Gibbons used this case as an example of the jurisdictional pressures OTA faced. He said, "This is an example, gentlemen, of one of the problems we get into when we try to work for all the committees of Congress. The number of committees of interest expanded, and so did the seeming scope of the work, and as time went on, we began to understand that some committees had an interest in a very broad study that would take a considerable amount of time. Others felt that a much more narrowly focused study would be best."[3] Ironically, the ANWR study encountered further problems when Senator Stevens of Alaska, still a board member, objected to any study at all, out of concern that the findings would be harmful to oil revenues in his state.

Sometimes, maneuvering among committees over the content of studies was more subtle. The agency's correspondence files were filled with letters from committees jockeying with one another for advantage over future bills that might be associated with a policy study. An illustrative example involved the Convention on the Regulation of Antarctic Mineral Resource Activities, which was signed in June 1988. As Congress prepared implementing legislation for the treaty, the Commerce Committee in the Senate wrote OTA, beginning with an assertion of jurisdiction over activities in the Antarctic of the National Science Foundation and the National Oceanographic and Atmospheric Administration, and requesting a study. The committee asked whether the treaty would limit the activities of its agencies, whether it would provide adequate environmental protection for the Antarctic, and whether firms that might wish to develop resources there would be adversely affected. [4]

The next month, the House Foreign Affairs Committee weighed in, stating its jurisdiction over activities of the State Department, and requesting that OTA assess the effects of the treaty on U.S. "national interests" in the region.[5] Only a day later came the House Merchant Marine Committee, with Jones asserting that his committee expected "to be involved in the development of implementing legislation" for the treaty, and posing a list of questions about the feasibility of developing resources in the Antarctic, the probability of an oil spill, and how various federal institutions would be involved in meeting the obligations of the study.[6]

Other legislators used an even lighter touch. Here are Senators Patrick Leahy and Richard Lugar of the Senate Agriculture Committee, writing to OTA on a study of pesticides in food: "We understand that Congressman John Dingell requested that the Office of Technology Assessment [perform a study of this issue, and] we would like to join in requesting this study and would appreciate being kept informed of its progress."[7] From Leahy and Lugar's perspective, participating in the sponsorship of OTA research offered several benefits. One was advance notice of findings that might be unfavorable, with the opportunity to minimize political damage by disavowing the report as soon as it was released. Another advantage was a little protection against inadvertently ceding leadership on the issue to Dingell, since such leadership is sometimes a function of being the first to be associated with a problem. For example, a staffer on the Democrat-controlled Senate Environment Committee explained that when her committee learned of proposed studies on topics relevant to its interests, it would invariably provide its own add-on request. When asked why, she said, "in order to frame the questions." She said, "We've sought to be in on clean air work where Dingell is involved, because his committee's view of clean air and ours is different."

Other committees echo this logic. A staff member of a House committee explained to me that when he learned of another committee's request for a study, he would call OTA in order "to determine if there is a jurisdictional problem" with the research. When there was, he said his committee would issue its own request, "in order to re-shape or re-focus the proposed study to meet our needs." For instance, when another committee requested an assessment of Superfund site cleanup progress, his committee jumped into the research process: "They have a tenuous jurisdictional interest in this . . . we looked at their letter [to OTA] and felt it impinged on our turf, so we issued our own request trying to change the focus." He said, "you have to have the ability to shape the study to fit the needs of the committee—framing the nature of the report is the issue."

Staff in most committee offices reported the same view. One said, "We would not . . . want OTA to work with Armed Services on hazardous waste at military sites. The results would be tailored to them. We would want to be involved to broaden the scope and have OTA pronounce on general standards [for waste disposal]." The same staffer said there were two reasons his committee requested studies from OTA. The first was where it "truly needs some help" and was "genuinely seeking technical assistance," while the second was "where other committees are involved, and you don't want to be left out. You don't want . . . another committee working with OTA on an issue in your jurisdiction."

A House Science Committee staffer explained that failing to join another committee's sponsorship of OTA research could "give the impression that we've ceded jurisdiction" on the issue. An analyst on the Budget Committee observed that the authorizing committees sometimes used OTA "to create an ownership stake." A Senate Energy Committee staffer said, "committees like Government Operations don't have [natural policy] jurisdiction, so OTA helps them get into issues." Another Senate staffer said that an add-on request to OTA was "just a signal to the other committee that we are going to be involved." When his committee learned that Sen. John Glenn of the Government Operations Committee had issued a request to OTA on Superfund, it issued its own request because it "didn't want it to look like [Government Operations] were out ahead."

It should be made clear that these committee staff were not describing changes in formal jurisdiction—the stakes in such battles were far too high for OTA to have influence. The process in which they used OTA was more nuanced, involving the posturing, leading, feinting, and seizing initiative that defines much of the early stages of the legislative process. As a House staffer said, "You can't expand your jurisdiction or change it by requesting an OTA report, but what [you] can do is say that within your jurisdiction— which may overlap with others—you are a player. . . . An OTA request can function as a signal to other committees that the requester intends to be active on an issue." One respondent in my interviews summed up his colleagues' comments well: "Turf is perception—you don't want to be perceived as being left out of something that turns out to be big," and getting in on the ground floor of a study by OTA was one small and inexpensive form of insurance against being left out.

When studies were released by OTA, a similar process of jockeying often took place. Committees maneuvered to position themselves for credit-claiming and publicity. As an aide to the Transportation Subcommittee of the House Science Committee explained, "if we send a letter, we get consulted on the release, and this is important because timing is everything in Congress." A House Agriculture Committee staffer said that being in on the release of a report from OTA "allows you to control an issue's spin some, allows you to posture to the press, to the public, the rest of Congress." Another House staffer said that when you had the right to release a report you could use a hearing "to grill OTA on a finding you disagree with" in order to "spin the release of the report your way."

The politics of jurisdiction in Congress represented for OTA another face to the problem of maintaining neutrality, and the agency found it could readily adapt its strategy of neutrality to this set of issues. The agency often found it "difficult to even tell which is the committee of primary jurisdiction," as an agency employee involved in congressional relations put it. OTA found that offering something for everyone would minimize conflict and criticism. According to John Gibbons, the agency's policy of inclusion evolved over time, as OTA faced larger numbers of stakeholders in each issue. By the early 1980s it became clear that unless the agency consulted several committees in each chamber, a study ran a high risk of "blindsiding" a committee chair—a basic breach of congressional etiquette. So the agency adopted the practice of informing all potentially interested committees of its plans for research. It went so far as to explicitly solicit contributions to the framing and release of its studies from all relevant committees. The agency often contacted four or five committees with notification of study requests. Committees sometimes found OTA staff quite aggressive about covering the political bases in this way. One House staffer explained that OTA would approach his committee and say, "Do you guys want to join in?," while another noted that OTA was often quite blunt, saying, "Someone's nosing around in your turf—do you care?"

The combination of committees' increasing interest in one another's involvement with OTA and the agency's solicitations of multiple requests is visible in data on the number of committees sponsoring each study. In the 1970s, most of the agency's studies were undertaken for a single committee. By the end of the agency's life, its studies averaged almost three committee sponsors each. Figure 1 shows the trend in the broadening of committee sponsorship of policy studies, a result of both increasing interest in OTA's work and the agency's self-protective solicitousness of sponsorship.

OTA employed other tactics to sustain its neutral stance. It coordinated press releases of its studies, so that all sponsoring committees could have an opportunity to participate. In instances where more than one committee wanted the right to release a report, OTA would arrange for separate simultaneous releases, so that each committee could indulge itself equally in spinning the findings.

It also employed a panel review system to good effect in the search for political balance. For each study, OTA convened a panel of fifteen to twenty reviewers, to provide guidance and review of the project. The panels did not simply provide the kind of technical review used in academia to vet schol-

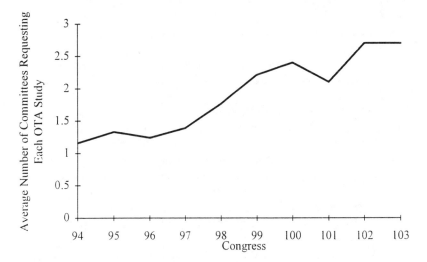

Figure 1. Building an Internal Constituency

arship. The panels served a role in political representation. Each was designed to include all politically interested parties in addition to providing
technical review. OTA's *Catching Our Breath: Next Steps for Reducing Urban Ozone*, which the Senate Environment Committee and House Energy
and Commerce Committee used in preparing the Clean Air Act Amendments
of 1990, was a good example. The panel included representatives of the
Natural Resources Defense Council, the American Lung Association, Ford
Motor Company, Proctor & Gamble, regional regulatory agencies, and universities. Panels like this one helped ensure that OTA had not overlooked a
committee chair's interests, and expanded the group of legislators who could
find a constituent or favored group whose ideas were represented in each
study.

The tactic for which OTA was best known was avoiding making policy recommendations. This practice was the foundation of its strategy of
neutrality: in almost every case, OTA refused to endorse specific congressional action. It provided a range of policy options, and presented arguments for
and against each, but carefully avoided recommending action.

In doing so, OTA clearly sacrificed the short-term influence over specific policies that would have come from staking out a position. In those rare
instances where a combination of the question it was asked and the evidence
it uncovered led it unavoidably to a policy position—on gun control and the
Strategic Defense Initiative, for instance—OTA indeed found its studies
bearing unusual weight. But in the long run, such recommendations would
have created a more vocal group of detractors than supporters.

OTA carried its effort to avoid policy positions to sometimes awkward
lengths. In a study of cooperation with the Soviet Union in energy development, where congressional opinion was unusually evenly divided, OTA split
three policy options that emerged from its research into four, because it
feared inadvertently suggesting that the middle option was somehow a logical compromise. In a hearing on MX missile basing, an analyst showed how
far OTA would go to evade questions about its "position." In the hearing,
OTA analyst Peter Sharfman offered standard OTA fare consisting of a neutral list of policy options. After listening to the testimony, Rep. Beverly
Byron asked Sharfman to render an informed opinion about how Congress
should proceed—the sort of invitation that is the dream of most policy analysts hoping their work will have an impact on politics. But Sharfman declined, following OTA practice by refusing to endorse any one of the alternatives OTA had proposed. When Byron insisted that he make a
recommendation, Sharfman found political cover by politely asking the chair
of the hearing for permission to refuse the request. With the chair's approval,
Sharfman withheld his opinion, prompting Byron to walk out of the hearing
in frustration.[8]

These practices—jurisdictional balancing, building coalitions through advisory panels, avoiding recommendations—paid off by the late 1980s in a remarkably favorable set of attitudes on and off the Hill toward the agency. By the early 1990s, committee chairs from both parties and their staffs went on record in support of the quality and bipartisanship of OTA's work. What limited press coverage OTA received was favorable, and the agency no longer encountered the kind of harsh editorials by conservatives it had elicited in the 1970s. An external review of Congress conducted jointly by the American Enterprise Institute and the Brookings Institution in 1993 found that "the agency is considered highly credible by members of both parties and is well regarded for its technical competence."[9] In interviews with me, a number of staff commented that their committees turned to OTA for information when they did not know whom else to believe, precisely because the agency was more neutral and credible than lobbyists, executive agencies, and even private think tanks who offer Congress advice. OTA had developed into one of the most well-respected analysts of policy in the country.

These endorsements reflect a remarkable shift from the widespread perceptions of politicization at OTA prior to the reforms begun by Russell Peterson. Between 1972 and the early 1990s, OTA did exactly what captive organizations of experts in government have traditionally been expected not to do: grow less politicized and more broadly credible. The explanation is consistent with the idea that there is a connection between the degree of centralization of authority in an institution and the degree of politicization of its captive experts. The implications of this connection did not escape OTA Director John Gibbons, who observed about OTA, "our survival depends on our being able to satisfy all the stakeholders in Congress."[10] In 1995 Republican Senator Orrin Hatch summarized OTA's experience, noting that the agency overcame its early biases, and remarking that "my recent experience has been that OTA is objective and bipartisan because it cannot afford not to be."[11]

OTA had used its strategy of neutrality to good effect. By the time of Hatch's comment, OTA could best be described as a modest agency providing policy expertise to a small but committed clientele of Republicans and Democrats. It avoided controversy while courting the support of committee chairs and ranking minority members. Its work was well respected among these primary constituents, as well as among policy analysts outside Congress, but it had never become particularly well known in the mass media or even among rank-and-file legislators—a byproduct of its strategy. In its laser-like emphasis on neutrality and balance, it had never emphasized external visibility, growth in budget and staffing, expansion of its role, or other elements of institutionalization. Given the structural and fiscal stability of the internal congressional environment of the 1980s, goals of that nature were secondary to the achievement of political accord. Unfortunately for the agency and its supporters, the election of 1994 brought a precipitous change in stability of the congressional environment. In one sense, OTA was prepared for Republican control of public policy; it had friends in the party and had established that it was no longer an instrument of Democratic policy. But is was not prepared for what was coming—a crusade by legislators to reorganize Congress, reduce its budget, and fire staff.

Chapter 7

Abolishing OTA: Budget Politics in the 104th Congress

O TA came to an abrupt end in 1995. In the space of a few months, the agency went from being a placid and uncontroversial resource for committees to a sacrifical lamb on the budget-cutter's chopping block. In one-third of the time OTA might have taken to study the advantages and disadvantages of abolishing an agency, it found its appropriation "zeroed-out" for fiscal year 1996.

OTA was caught up in the "Republican Revolution" through the effort to balance the budget, although its termination was no more than a footnote to budget and appropriations battles that followed the election of 1994. The legislative branch appropriation received special attention from Republican budget-cutters in the 104th Congress. At around $2.4 billion, the congressional appropriation consumed on the order of one-tenth of one percent of a federal budget that would have had to be cut by about ten percent to balance. Firing the entire legislature and all its staff, and returning its appropriation to the Treasury would scarcely have made a noticeable mark on the budget deficit.

But the symbolic value of cutting the congressional budget outweighed the direct monetary worth of the exercise. There was a widespread sense among legislators in 1995 that deficit reduction should "start at home," that Congress should demonstrate its willingness to make sacrifices along with the rest of the nation. In the words of Rep. Dave Weldon of Florida, "we need to show good faith and cut our own staff."[1] Ron Packard of California, chair of the Legislative Branch Subcommittee of House Appropriations said: "We think it's important that the Congress sends the message that we're downsizing our agencies and ourselves, and we expect the rest of the government to fall in line."[2] A witness at a joint House-Senate budget hearing in early 1995 used the term, "getting [Congress'] own house in order," to describe the same idea.[3] David Mason, director of the Heritage Foundation's U.S. Congress Assessment Project, told members that whatever small contribution toward deficit reduction Congress could make by reducing its own spending would be "magnified many times by its value as an example."[4]

On the House side of Capitol Hill, written into the Contract with America were reductions in staff sizes and a major audit of Congress for the old nemesis of good government, "waste, fraud or abuse." But it was in the Senate that Republicans took the lead in developing a specific plan for trimming Congress. In December 1994, within a month of the election that gave them majority status, the Republican Conference passed a resolution on congressional reform, stating the party's belief that it was imperative that the legislative branch be reduced in size and cost as a signal of budget leadership in a period when nearly every aspect of the federal government was to be trimmed. The conference labeled the idea "Cutting Congress First."[5] The resolution called for a fifteen percent reduction in committees' budgets, a 12.5 percent reduction in leadership and support offices, and substantial reductions in the cost of the four congressional support agencies, including a twenty-five percent reduction at GAO and abolition of OTA altogether.

The GAO and OTA cuts were championed by Senator Connie Mack, Conference Secretary, who was in line to become chair of the Legislative Branch Appropriations Subcommittee. At a time when both parties were still stunned by the outcome of the election, and most legislators' attention was turned to Speaker Newt Gingrich's Contract, the resolution passed with little discussion or debate in the Conference.

Mack and Senator Peter Domenici then formed a Working Group on Congressional Reform to expand upon the resolution. Their group produced thirty-two recommendations, including the adoption of a two-year budget and appropriations cycle and streamlining of the committees. The group gave a good deal of attention to changes in congressional staff and support agencies, which accounted for nearly half the legislature's budget.[6] Trimming congressional agencies provided an alternative to cuts in legislators' personal staffs and other sources closer to home. The Senate group proposed repealing permanent authorizations for GAO, CBO, CRS, and the Government Printing Office in favor of eight-year authorizations, and creating a cost-accounting and voucher system for rationing the services of the agencies.

The group also endorsed the proposal for eliminating OTA that was in the Conference document, and supported the cut at GAO. Trimming GAO by twenty-five percent would save about $100 million from the legislative branch appropriation. But abolishing OTA would save only about $20 million—a tiny amount even with respect to just the legislative budget.

So why choose OTA for elimination? The agency was actually a logical choice given legislators' desire for symbolic cuts in Congress. It represented a concrete budget prize whose significance was potentially greater than $20 million. "Zeroing out" OTA would allow legislators to advertise that a congressional agency had been eliminated outright. Staff on the Hill referred to this strategy variously, with terms like "trophy hunting," "building moral capital," and "demonstrating budget-cutting *bona fides.*"

The cost to legislators would not be high. OTA's contribution to the policy process was not as well formalized or institutionalized as that of its sibling agencies. Losing its annual output of thirty studies was not something that most members would feel immediately. Compared to dropping other items from the legislative budget outright, the effects of eliminating OTA paled. The Congressional Budget Office, for instance, was roughly the same size as OTA in budget and staff, but its elimination would clearly diminish Congress's capacity to wield the power of the purse, and would be felt by many members. OTA's constituency, on the other hand, was comparatively small and the agency's absence would not directly hamper any area of policy-making. The committee chairs and ranking minority members were those most directly connected with its studies—most members had little contact with the agency. New freshmen in particular knew little or nothing of the agency's work.

So OTA found itself the target of a serious effort to reduce the size of Congress. OTA had spent years crafting its strategy of neutrality. That had meant mainly avoiding making enemies and staying away from controversy. But it had not entailed building a large constituency of supporters who relied on it and who in turn could be relied on to defend it. For twenty years, OTA had outfitted itself against charges of bias. It was comparatively well suited to defend itself in that connection. But it was not well equipped for the kind of attack being mounted.

A wave of public criticism of Republican tax and welfare proposals in March only strengthened the resolve of Mack and other Republicans to terminate OTA. A Republican aide in the Senate close to the process took pains to explain to me that the attack on OTA's budget was not a reprise of party challenges to the agency's credibility from years earlier. "This is not a partisan thing," he claimed, "we stipulate that OTA does great science. They are widely and globally recognized and cited." But, he said, "We're talking about taking away school lunches . . . we have to look pretty hard at their $20 million budget." Rep. George Brown, Democrat of California and a long-time agency supporter, explained that OTA was a small, easily targeted agency whose elimination would have an adverse effect on Congress's long-range well-being, but would not have any direct, short-term consequences for legislators' interests. [7]

The scientific and technical community outside Congress mobilized to convince Mack and others of the agency's worth, but their efforts had little effect. Mack argued that Congress could not afford OTA in times of lean budgets, not that the agency did poor work. The arguments of academics that OTA was a credible, unbiased agency performing good analysis had little force against Mack's claim. Even staff at OTA acknowledged that it was difficult to object to a legislator who said that OTA's services were not necessary to him. This was a contingency for which OTA was not well prepared.

On the Hill, OTA's small group of allies in each party rallied. Democrat John Dingell called OTA a "valuable asset," and observed that "no such bipartisan agency could exist in the executive branch."[8] Republican Mike Oxley described having relied on OTA to resolve conflicting technical claims by the telephone industry and the FBI, and urged his colleagues to retain the agency for just such situations, where Congress was confronted by conflicting experts.[9]

Some defenders of the agency invoked the venerable argument that had been made when Congress had debated creating OTA, decades earlier. Referring to OTA as the only independent source of technical expertise available to Congress, Representative Vic Fazio said, "The Department of Energy will tell you [their policy] is the greatest thing since sliced bread. We need someone who will tell you the opposite."[10] In the Senate, Ernest Hollings argued that OTA was a "shared congressional resource." He said that "science and technology issues are increasingly intertwined with the issues of the day, whether it be health, telecommunications, national security, or the environment. Some critics of OTA recognize its utility but call it a luxury we cannot afford in these times. This is nonsense. In this era, we need more common resources not fewer. In particular, we need help condensing the vast amount of information out there, sorting out what is important and what is not, and presenting it to us in an unbiased and objective manner. Without such a resource, we will continue to rely more and more on the executive branch for information about science and technology—this is exactly the spot we were in over twenty years ago that gave impetus to creating OTA."[11]

Orrin Hatch urged his colleagues not to "cut off our nose to spite our faces," saying, "I do not believe that anyone who knows anything about science and technology seriously questions the quality of OTA's work nor the agency's credibility. We cannot afford to rely exclusively on the limited executive agency analyses of technology development and R&D needs."

Hatch urged that OTA bear its proportional share of budget reductions, but not be abolished altogether.[12]

Had the attack on the agency's $20 million come at another period in Congress' history, it would have posed a much more tractable problem for these supporters. But with nearly every other line item in the federal budget also marked for reduction, and historic battles still pending over welfare, health care, the environment, taxes, the structure of federalism, and on and on, even some OTA supporters did not make saving the agency a top priority.

The budget resolution for fiscal year 1996 formalized the proposal to terminate OTA, as one small element in the monumental plan to balance the budget in seven years. Accompanying their resolutions, both budget committees released "hit lists" of agencies proposed for elimination. In the House, OTA joined a dozen executive branch and independent agencies and three cabinet departments marked for termination.[13]

The situation in the appropriations committees did not bode well for the agency's supporters. In the Senate, Mack's chair-ship of the legislative branch subcommittee meant that the agency could expect a bill with no funding to come out of mark-up, regardless of what happened in the House, and it would then be an uphill battle to defeat the subcommittee bill in the full committee. Unlike the situation in 1981 with Senator Mattingly, no OTA board members sat on the subcommittee, and a strong tide for trimming Congress was running.

The position of appropriators in the House was much more uncertain. Rep. Robert Livingston, chair of the Appropriations Committee, and Rep. Ron Packard, Mack's counterpart on the House Legislative Branch Subcommittee, were noncommittal, revealing no position on the proposal being pushed by Mack. Throughout the Spring the chair of OTA's authorizing committee, Robert Walker, also avoided committing himself either to defending the agency's appropriation or to joining with those seeking its elimination. This public ambiguity in the House sparked a good deal of speculation at the agency: perhaps there was disagreement in the House about what to do with OTA, or the leadership had not taken a position. In any case, silence in the House focused most of the efforts of OTA's defenders on Senator Mack, until the House eventually took up the legislative branch appropriation bill in Summer.

On June 8, the House subcommittee chaired by Packard reported a bill on a voice vote that "zeroed" the agency's funding. About two weeks later, the full committee reported essentially the same bill to the floor, signaling that the House leadership was indeed supportive of terminating OTA. The language in the Appropriations Committee report was terse in its treatment of the OTA funding:

The Committee has not provided funds for the Office of Technology Assessment. If any functions of OTA must be retained, they shall be assumed by other agencies such as Congressional Research Service or the General Accounting Office. Alternatively, the National Academy of Sciences, university research programs, and a variety of private sector institutions will be available to supplement the needs of Congress for objective, unbiased technology assessments.[14]

After the committee vote, supporters of the agency met to devise a floor strategy. Republican Amo Houghton and Democrats John Dingell, George Brown, and Vic Fazio designed a plan with two amendments. Fazio would offer language restoring $18.6 million to the agency, and Houghton would then offer a friendly substitute that transferred OTA's functions into the Congressional Research Service, and shifted $15 million in funding from the Library of Congress for the operation of OTA inside CRS. It was clear that members would not support the original amendment, but the group hoped that Houghton's amendment might prevail by appearing modest in contrast. It offered the chance to keep the total legislative appropriation at the level set by the committee, let legislators claim to have eliminated OTA as an agency, and yet preserve most of its staff and functions as a division of CRS. Not only would the double-amendment approach make the Houghton plan seem temperate by comparison with the Fazio plan, it would buy agency supporters an extra ten minutes of debate under the floor rule.

What ensued surprised everyone, and showed that even comparatively small issues can precipitate major legislative brawls. The first vote in the full House, which came on June 21, was on substituting Houghton's amendment for Fazio's. To the delight of the agency, the amendment prevailed by a vote of 228–201. Forty-eight Republicans had joined with 180 Democrats, and agency supporters read in this outcome an endorsement of OTA. Among committee chairs, eight supported the agency and twelve voted against it, along with the majority leader and whip. If the amendment could survive, then OTA might reasonably hope that a compromise in conference with even the worst possible Senate bill might leave the agency with $5–10 million. The effect on the agency would be huge, but funds might be gradually re-accumulated in future appropriations cycles.

After that first vote, the House took up the question of adopting the amended Fazio amendment. But this time the outcome was very different, reflecting whip pressure by the Republican leadership, which successfully mobilized party members between the two votes. Twenty-one Republicans, including three committee chairs, dropped their support of OTA between the first and second votes, while the agency managed to pick up only a few

Democrats to compensate. At end of the seventeen-minute voting period, the presiding officer, John Linder of Georgia, "called the vote," leaving OTA with a cliffhanger loss of 213–214.

But it was not quite over. Precisely what happened next is a matter of dispute. Minority Whip David Bonior rose, saying to Linder, "the gentleman in the chair, respectfully I say to him, called the vote while two of our members were voting. That, Mr. Chairman, is not fair. It is not right. This side of the aisle is not going to stand for it."[15]

The period for electronic voting had ended, but in the House, members who miss the end of electronic voting may vote manually by entering the well at the front of the floor and handing the clerk a voting card—as long as the presiding officer has not yet officially endèd—"called"—the vote. By tradition, the presiding officer of the House delays calling a vote if a member is in the well in the process of voting. Bonior asserted that two Democrats, Thomas Foglietta and Earl Hilliard, had been in that situation and had been denied the opportunity to cast the winning votes. When Linder rejected Bonior's claim, the floor erupted with Democrats shouting, "Shame, Shame." The House adjourned for the day with minority members in an uproar.

The first order of business the next day was the disputed ruling. Majority Leader Richard Armey spoke first, telling his colleagues that he had reviewed the videotape of the previous day's proceedings, and found nothing out of order. He said that the tape "showed the well of the House was empty of members" when the vote was ended, and then "after some time two Members from the minority party appeared at the desk and attempted to vote." Moreover, Armey noted, a third member, a Republican, followed the Democrats, and he too had not been allowed to vote. Had all three voted, the outcome would have remained the same, since the amendment would fail on a tie vote. Having said that, Armey went on to note that "it is also true that many Members, most especially members on this side of the aisle who supported the Houghton language earlier, felt that their victory had been snatched from them."[16] In light of what Armey called the difficulty of overcoming perceptions of unfairness even in the face of facts, he would make the extraordinary move of asking unanimous consent that the disputed vote be vacated and a new vote immediately held.

Minority Leader Richard Gephardt rose to assert that the Democratic version of events was different, that the members were indeed on the floor and were attempting to cast their votes. He remarked, "I have been here now 19 years, and I have not in my experience seen the depth of feeling" generated by the controversy.[17] Foglietta and Hilliard themselves then spoke, stating that they had been attempting to approach the well, but were unable physically to reach the desk in time. Foglietta claimed that *The Washington Post* had timed the sequence of events and found that Linder had called the vote fifteen seconds short of the allotted seventeen minutes, while Hilliard denied that a third Republican legislator had followed them.

A series of hostile, partisan, one-minute speeches followed the statements by Foglietta and Hilliard. Democratic Whip Bonior called the event the day before "the most egregious and arrogant abuse of power that I have seen on our House floor."[18] Several Democrats charged that Republicans had been hasty in order to depart for a fundraising event in New York City that had netted party members $1.7 million. Republican Joe Scarborough charged Democrats with demagoguery.

Nonetheless, Armey's request to vacate the disputed vote brought no objections, and so a third vote on OTA funds was brought. And again the outcome was a reversal of the preceding vote. By a vote of 220–204, the House adopted the Houghton-Fazio amendment, restoring OTA funding and consolidating the agency into CRS. The agency had picked up votes from more Democrats who had voted against it previously, as well as from some Republicans, like William Goodling and Pat Roberts, who had voted for OTA the first time, switched positions in the second vote, and then changed back to voting in favor of the OTA funds in the third round.

So OTA had avoided outright termination in the House, but only under the most unusual of circumstances. The nature of the vote did not leave agency supporters in a strong position to influence the Senate vote or enter conference negotiations. In the Senate, the movement against the agency went more smoothly, where resolve to de-fund it was stronger and the influence of Senator Mack greater. Agency supporters tried an amendment strategy similar to the one used in the House. In the Appropriations Committee, Ernest Hollings offered an amendment to restore funding at the $15 million level by reducing the appropriations of other congressional agencies by a small fraction. The plan was an adaptation of Houghton's amendment. In the House, the Librarian of Congress had objected vociferously to reducing the Library's appropriation in order to fund the whole of OTA's shift into CRS. So Hollings' bill found money for OTA by assessing the Library and other agencies by just one percent each. The amendment was intended to demonstrate how inexpensive OTA was, but instead it showed how committed legislators were to abolishing it. The committee rejected the money-shifting plan 11–13, and signalled to OTA that things would likely not go well on the floor. Hollings re-offered his amendment on the floor on July 20, but it met a similar fate. Senators tabled it by a vote of 54–45, leaving the appropriations bill with only enough funding for OTA to finish work presently underway and then close its doors. On the floor OTA had attracted the votes of ten Republicans who disagreed with Mack—six of them committee chairs—but it lost ten Democrats sold on the idea of creating a symbol of budget-cutting.

In conference, there wasn't the compromise OTA supporters had hoped for. House conferees acceded to the Senate provisions on OTA, setting the close of fiscal year 1995 as the end of OTA's operations. The final legislative branch bill appropriated $2.19 billion for Congress, a reduction of about $206 million from the previous year. The bill gave OTA employees sixty days of severance pay, and provided for a close-out team of seventeen to work into the new fiscal year to shut down the agency's operations. After the vote, agency Director Roger Herdman vowed to remain among the skeleton staff boxing up the agency's records and to personally turn out the lights for the last time.[19]

In the end, OTA's funding was eliminated not because it was too large, but because it was so tiny. Terminating the agency did not require Congress to absorb the loss of a large or well institutionalized operation. It offered a small real contribution to budget reduction and seemed to provide a larger symbol of congressional commitment to reducing the size of government. Ironically, that effort at symbolism eventually failed. Legislators lost control of the "Cutting Congress First" message in the media, which tended to portray the elimination of OTA as either an act of short-sightedness or simply the ending of a congressional perk—akin to free ice-deliveries and subsidized haircuts. When the end of the fiscal year arrived and Congress had passed only one other appropriation bill, President Clinton chided legislators for taking care of Congress first while failing to fund the rest of the government. In the end it is doubtful whether legislators reaped any "moral capital" from the whole excercise. OTA's life span was thus bracketed by two major periods of change in Congress, the reforms of the 1970s at its beginning, and, at its end, the changes of the 90s begun in the election of 1994.

Chapter 8

The Other Congressional Support Agencies

Chapter 2 suggested that there is good reason to believe that the traditional account of "neutral competence" and the politicization of expertise is only a special case of a broader connection between political structure and the politicization of expertise. We saw that political institutions could be expected to elicit a range of politically committed or politically neutral knowledge from captive experts, depending upon the organization of power within them. Decentralization and pluralistic arrangements of power led one to expect the Congress of the 1970s and 1980s to tend to reward neutral expertise, while more centralized, hierarchical executive agencies—as well as the White House itself—should tend to reward politicized expertise.

The case of OTA's rise in the 1970s and fall in 1995 is consistent with this expectation. The agency's strategy of neutrality emerged as an explicit accommodation to the nature of power in Congress, after a period of experimentation with other approaches. The well-meaning exhortations of OTA's creators—Harvey Brooks, Emilio Daddario, and others—that the new agency provide neutral expertise proved a failure in OTA's initial years. But the incentives to develop a sustainable relationship with those in power—Republicans, Democrats, and a multiplicity of committee chairs—succeeded where good wishes failed, producing an agency that grew more credible and less politicized the longer it was exposed to congressional politics.

But of course despite its good fit to the theory, OTA is just one case. Before concluding that OTA's experiences verify a general feature of the politics of expertise, evidence whether this case is typical or not is in order. It could be fortuitousness in the selection of OTA as a case study that the evidence presented in the preceding chapters is consistent with expectations about the politics of expertise in Congress. OTA was one of four agencies or "instrumentalities" of Congress whose mission was to provide expertise, and it is important to have some measure of whether the cases of the other three are consistent with that of OTA.

Was OTA's strategy of neutrality the product of unique circumstances, or does it indeed reflect a more general feature of expertise in a decentralized institution? If the relationship that developed between legislators and the experts at OTA is a product of a general set of political dynamics in Congress, then the experiences of other congressional agencies should be similar. The Congressional Research Service, the Congressional Budget Office, and the General Accounting Office provide expertise and information to Congress under much the same institutional circumstances as did OTA. These support offices can provide a means of checking on inferences about Congress drawn from OTA.

First impressions suggest that the agencies could not be more different. CBO is a creation and servant of the budget process in Congress, and has an institutionalized role in cost scoring, forecasting, and budget analysis. CRS, a part of the Library of Congress, serves mainly as a reference librarian and staff aide to legislators, providing facts and figures, assisting with speech-writing, and so on. GAO, on the other hand, was once an executive branch office, then a quasi-independent agency, and now undertakes oversight and program evaluation as a congressional support office. None of the agencies has a board of directors like OTA's, or appears at first to share much in common organizationally. Yet beneath the external differences one can readily identify a very similar set of strategies for responding to decentralized control and heterogenous demands for information.

THE CONGRESSIONAL RESEARCH SERVICE

CRS is a good place to begin a comparison between OTA and the other congressional agencies. CRS is by far the least well known publicly of the three agencies now serving Congress in an expert capacity. CRS focuses on meeting congressional needs in a direct and often private way, and much of its activity is invisible outside of Capitol Hill. Some of CRS's work is performed in confidence for individual legislators, so at times even colleagues on the Hill do not know what information and assistance the agency is providing. In fact, CRS is officially forbidden from publicly distributing most of its documents, so while a report from CBO or GAO might be widely read and discussed in Washington, CRS's activities are chiefly the domain of staff and legislators themselves.

CRS is part of the Library of Congress, but it functions quasi-autonomously from the rest of the Library and is therefore generally treated as an independent agency of Congress. It is different from OTA in important ways. One of the most significant differences is the volume of requests for assistance CRS receives from Congress, and the time dedicated to each request. Whereas OTA responded to only a few dozen requests for information each year, CRS is deluged with roughly one-half *million* annually. OTA studies typically required about two years to complete; CRS responds to two-thirds of its half-million requests within twenty-four hours, and ninety percent within one week. With a budget of about $60 million and roughly a thousand employees, CRS is several times larger than OTA was in its final year.

CRS's volume of activity indicates how different the character of most of its work is from the comprehensive analysis performed at OTA. CRS is in many ways a Grand Central Station of information, where a ceaseless schedule of questions arrive and are routed to the appropriate experts. These experts draw on the published literature and resources of the Library of Congress, and rely on their own expertise to refer answers back to Congress as rapidly as possible. About two-thirds of these answers are factual in nature, allowing for the agency's quick response. The remainder involve what CRS labels "policy analysis," and require more preparation, analysis, or writing on the part of agency staff. The range of services and material CRS provides Congress is far greater than that of any of the other agencies, including OTA. CRS even offers language translation for legislators and orientation programs for new staff.

Unlike OTA, whose resources were controlled by committees, CRS serves members, committees, and staff, and so has the broadest clientele of any of the support agencies. Approximately three-fifths of requests to the agency come from legislators' personal offices. A significant part of CRS's work involves constituency service for legislators, an activity that none of the other congressional agencies undertakes. CRS handles constituent mail by preparing packages of information and even cover letters if requested. About one-seventh of the requests reaching CRS involve such inquiries.[1]

CRS also dedicates a significant amount of effort to self-initiated work described as "prior" to requests. This prior work is intended to anticipate congressional needs. For instance, the agency might prepare a summary of overnight developments in an overseas crisis so that legislators have briefing materials available when they arrive at their offices in the morning. Although only about one percent of "requests" numerically are self-initiated, these consume nearly one-quarter of CRS staff time.[2]

Despite these differences in the character of their activities, CRS exhibits many similarities to OTA in its adaptations to the congressional environment. While its roots are much older, its development has important parallels with that of OTA. The agency's origins date to 1914, when Congress created the Legislative Reference Service (LRS) within the Library of Congress. The purpose of the new department, created at the urging of Senator Robert LaFollette, Sr., was to make the Library's many resources more accessible to legislators. The Legislative Reorganization Act of 1946 significantly expanded LRS, giving it statutory authorization for the first time, and endorsing its role as a congressional ally. When it was preparing the reform act, the Joint Committee on the Organization of Congress, known then as the LaFollette-Monroney Committee, used the 32-year-old LRS as a vehicle for strengthening Congress' powers with respect to the executive branch. As one of the agency's own analysts writes, many legislators were worried that Congress was losing its status as a co-equal branch of government, and sought to improve the quality of staff resources as one form of response.[3] Legislators were even self-conscious about the stature of congressional staff with respect to executive branch employees, and set out an explicit "parity principle" for pay, so that LRS staff at all levels would be paid comparably to their executive branch counterparts.

Desire for parity in a larger sense produced another round of institution-building at CRS a few decades later, in the form of the Legislative Reorganization Act of 1970. The Joint Committee on the Organization of Congress again used LRS as a vehicle for strengthening Congress' hand with respect to the executive branch. The bill expanded the Service, and, to reflect the aim of making Congress a capable producer of research rather than only a librarian for the nation, it also changed LRS's name to the Congressional Research Service. Former CRS Deputy Director William Robinson calls the Reorganization Act "the legislative declaration of analytic independence from the executive branch."[4]

During consideration of the 1970 act, debate over how LRS/CRS would be governed revealed legislators' concerns with institutional loyalty, responsiveness, and non-partisanship. The Joint Committee evaluated separating CRS from the Library of Congress, in order to guarantee its direct responsiveness to Congress. In the House Rules Committee, which called for a tripling of CRS's staff by 1975, legislators concurred with the goal of congressional loyalty, but felt that the separation of CRS from the Library might subject it to greater politicization.[5] The Committee argued that the Library served to insulate the Service from partisan pressures, and rejected the call for separation. The final bill provided that the CRS director be appointed by the Librarian of Congress, but subject to approval by the Joint

Committee on the Library—an accommodation to the dual demands for non-partisanship and institutional loyalty. It called for the director and assistant to be appointed "without reference to political affiliation."[6]

The goal of non-partisanship was fulfilled at CRS. The agency has achieved a reputation for balance and neutrality in its work, and it has the strongest reputation for non-partisanship of the congressional agencies. Complaints on Capitol Hill that CRS is politically biased are rare.

It earned its reputation for balance in several ways that go well beyond the modest political insulation afforded its director. Robinson writes that "CRS maintains a sharp focus on its only client, the Congress"—by which he means that CRS is responsive to both parties, all members, and every jurisdictional interest.[7] These words ring true to OTA Director John Gibbons's comment that OTA succeeds by "maintaining a careful focus on the clients."[8] Robinson also echoes Orrin Hatch's comments about OTA, saying that "objectivity and non-partisanship" are "not only functional but essential to the very survival of CRS."[9]

CRS earns some of its support in Congress through its services unrelated to specific policy issues. Its digest of congressional bills, constituent mail handling, seminars on the legislative process, language translation, and much of its reference work are easily separated from partisan politics and advocacy, being equally valuable to members of both parties and any ideological persuasion. These administrative services have helped institutionalize CRS as a nearly indispensable source of staff support to a wide constituency within Congress.

For dealing with requests from legislators about policy problems that might lead it into advocacy or charges of "bias," CRS has developed formal procedures and an organizational culture intended to demonstrate political neutrality—just as OTA did. CRS staff have adopted a norm of non-partisanship in their analysis of issues similar to that at OTA, using neutral language and constructs, and giving equal treatment to "pros" and "cons." And, like OTA, CRS operates within a strict policy of not offering policy recommendations, regardless of the inclinations of its experts. A reviewing office at CRS is dedicated to checking outgoing reports for balance and neutrality before they are delivered to a legislator or committee! These practices are intended to ensure that no legislator's position is slighted in a CRS document.

Often, the agency is asked by legislators to prepare material that is supportive of a particular position or political pursuit. This kind of request might involve preparation of material to be inserted in a committee report, or the drafting of language for a speech. These requests ask CRS to function as an advocate, and place it in a difficult position. It has adopted a tactic for remaining neutral in such situations while also assisting the legislator in his or her pursuit. The approach differs from that taken at OTA, but is very successful. Instead of attempting to expand the scope of the request to be inclusive of a variety of political perspectives, as OTA did, CRS adopts a veil of anonymity. It prepares the material from the member's political perspective, whatever that might be, and then removes all traces of its origin at CRS from the document. CRS labels the result "directed writing," in distinction to its standard neutral documentation, and it bears no author's name or CRS identification. The material is officially untraceable to the agency. CRS gets to have its cake and eat it too: it supports the legislator's political position while maintaining its official status as neutral. The use of "directed writing" guarantees that the only documentation circulated on Capitol Hill that is identifiable as CRS work is that which has been carefully crafted to be neutral.

These tactics at CRS amount to a strategy of neutrality much like that of OTA. Also born partly out of legislators' desire to maintain Congress's prerogatives against the executive branch, CRS is an exceptional example of neutral competence. Not only has it been able to sustain its relevance and utility across changes in party control and ideology in Congress, it has developed techniques for simultaneously supporting the informational demands of legislators of all stripes. Perhaps even more than OTA, CRS reveals the adaptive advantage of a strategy of expert neutrality in the legislature.

THE CONGRESSIONAL BUDGET OFFICE

Of all the congressional agencies, CBO bears the most striking marks of legislators' desire to maintain independence from the executive branch in policy expertise. Its creation by the Congressional Budget and Impoundment Control Act of 1974 made it part of that congressional revolution against White House power in budgeting. William Robinson's praise for the significance of CRS notwithstanding, the creation of CBO is an even better example of a "declaration of analytic independence" from the White House by Congress. CBO broke OMB's monopoly on budget information, and, as Wildavsky has noted, the competition the agency provides over budget estimation appears to provide a continuing impetus to accuracy in budget analysis.[10] Establishing CBO was easily the most direct attempt in congressional history to assert power over policy-making through control over experts. The agency has this *raison d'etre* in common with CRS and OTA.

Matters of neutrality at CBO are interesting indeed, and present a somewhat more complicated case than at CRS or OTA. Like OTA—and, for a while, during the same period—CBO experienced a rocky start, and has been the subject of charges of favoritism and advocacy. Also like OTA, CBO emerged from controversy through a strategy of neutrality and non-partisanship. In much of its work, the elements of CBO's strategy closely parallel OTA's. But the structure of some of CBO's work, namely budget forecasting, has made it much more difficult to avoid associating itself with specific policy positions. This fact fostered a low-grade but continual resentment among Republicans for some time.

In its first years, CBO struggled in a rather public way to define its role in policy-making. Between 1975 and, roughly, the end of the decade, it was plagued by charges of political bias. The origins of the charges were similar to those with which OTA wrestled: struggles between rival committees for control over the agency, and suspicion by some Republicans that the agency favored liberal interests.

CBO's early troubles derived from competing conceptions in Congress about its role. When the budget act was under consideration, members of the Rules Committee in the House wanted CBO to function in a narrowly defined way, serving strictly as a staff organization to the budget committees. In the Senate, members wanted an independent agency with a broader scope. These two views developed into distinct House and Senate perspectives on CBO.

The Senate conception of CBO involved better budget information being distributed throughout Congress, with a consequently broad diffusion of the power that can potentially come from knowledge. Many senators expected CBO to function like a Brookings Institution for Congress. The House perspective, on the other hand, pictured CBO as more like the staff of a joint committee. The advantages of better budget information would accrue mainly to the budget committees, not the institution as a whole.[11] These concerns in the House echoed representatives' fears from a few years earlier that the creation of OTA would undermine the authority of the committee chairs if too many members had access to agency resources.

The budget act provisions for CBO represented a compromise in classic legislative tradition. CBO was created as a separate agency, as preferred in the Senate, but was to answer primarily to the new budget committees also established by the act, in response to House concerns. CBO's priorities would be, first, to serve the House and Senate budget committees, then the appropriations and tax committees, and next, authorizing committees. Individual members could receive information from CBO, but were not intended to sponsor major studies.

The compromise did not end the conflict over CBO's role, and the dispute carried over into the agency's relationships with the budget committees, which sought different forms of assistance from the agency. In its first few years, CBO attempted to position itself as independent from direct committee control, and moved to establish the authority to make policy judgements and to speak directly to the public through the media. CBO's first director, Alice Rivlin, set a course for the agency that involved far more autonomy than either CRS or OTA enjoyed. Her view of the agency was akin to that of the Senate. CBO would be a comparatively independent operation providing more than just scorekeeping and forecasts. It would conduct policy analysis of a much broader scope. This strategy was much like that of Russell Peterson at OTA. The idea was to establish the agency as an independent think tank sponsored by the legislature. Rivlin did not hesitate to make statements directly to the media about budget policy, and by the end of 1975, had hired nearly two hundred staff at CBO without consulting the appropriations committees who would pay for them.

Legislators responded to CBO's attempt at independence just as they did OTA's under Peterson. A series of confrontations with members brought controversy to CBO, among charges that Rivlin was acting as a policy advocate rather than helping Congress do its work. Both Democrats and Republicans tangled with CBO, including OTA's enemy Elford Cederberg. In the House, for instance, Rep. Bauman complained that under Rivlin CBO was inappropriately involving itself in political matters, and Senator Bob Dole felt it necessary to remind CBO in its first year that its primary purpose was to respond to congressional needs rather than pursuing its own ideas and programs. Much of the criticism of CBO's independent style centered in the appropriations and budget committees, especially among conservatives, who argued that Rivlin was building CBO into a liberal policy institute. The House Appropriations Committee used the matter of Rivlin's staffing plans to go on the attack in late 1975, forcing her to defend the agency's role and her large staff against attempts to reduce CBO's size by half. As Schick notes in his history, the perception that CBO was pursuing its own policy agenda under Rivlin was widely unacceptable to legislators of all stripes.[12] The pressures on CBO were not simply partisan in nature, but involved a combination of institutional impulses, demands for greater political propriety of a general sort, and insistence by members of each party that CBO not favor the other.

CBO capitulated, adopting a lower profile that avoided policy advocacy and dropping explicitly self-initiated studies in favor of responding to requests. It also redoubled its commitment to non-partisanship, and relied on the same policy as OTA's regarding not making policy recommendations. By the time Rudolph Penner, a moderate Republican, replaced Rivlin in 1984, concern that the agency was not responsive enough to congressional interests had faded. Under Robert Reischauer and then June O'Neill, CBO has demonstrated its loyalty to Congress; no longer are questions raised about whether it is pursuing its own agenda or supporting the legislature's activities.

But the question of partisanship has been a difficult one for the agency. CBO has always found it advantageous to advertise neutrality, and CBO staff explain the value of this strategy in essentially the same terms as do CRS and OTA staff. Serving multiple principals among whom power is widely fragmented requires offering something for everyone. James Blum, an Assistant Director for Budget Analysis at CBO, explained that not only is CBO under written instructions from the appropriations committees to be neutral in its analyses, but "further impetus toward non-partisanship stems from the fact that CBO works for both Houses of Congress, each with its own tradition and mores, and serves both the majority and minority in each house."[13]

On matters of policy analysis, CBO has developed a well-known reputation for public ambivalence, casting policy alternatives in the language of "one the one hand, . . . on the other hand." CBO employees can sometimes be identified in Washington for no other trait than their familiarity with this construct. But on matters of budget forecasting, CBO has found it more difficult to convince some legislators of its commitment to neutrality, since the result of much of its work is numerical, and equivocation is more difficult. One of CBO's most important annual reports is its review of the President's budget proposals, which it typically issues in February or March. The agency re-estimates the president's budget figures using its own economic forecast and "technical" assumptions, producing competing estimates of revenues, outlays, and the deficit. During the twelve years of divided control from 1981–1993, CBO found it difficult to avoid the perception that its critiques of administration budget figures represented anything but the result of an alliance with congressional Democrats against Presidents Reagan and Bush.

CBO staunchly defends its neutrality by claiming its forecasts are more accurate than the President's, and it has offered data to support the claim.[14] OMB, under even stronger criticism that its budget figures are biased (in support of the President), defends itself as well. In the 1990 presidential budget document, for example, OMB noted that despite the "widespread, but mistaken view that its economic forecasts have been inaccurate because of excessive optimism," the data show that its near-term economic forecasts are as accurate as CBO's and those of private forecasters.[15]

Part of the dispute over who is more accurate or less biased stems from differences between deficit estimates and economic forecasts; both sides may be right. As OMB contends, neither organization is reliably more accurate than the other at long-range *economic* forecasting. But for estimating the size of the short-term *budget deficit,* arguably the most politically salient figure, data suggest that CBO indeed has stronger claim. Figure 2 shows a comparison of CBO and OMB errors in one-year deficit forecasts, based on the President's proposed policies. In nearly every forecast made since 1982, CBO has forecast a higher deficit than has OMB, and in nearly every case, CBO has been closer to the actual mark. While CBO has a significantly more *accurate* track record than OMB for this period, both agencies have been biased in favor of optimism, more often than not underestimating the size of the deficit.[16]

But perceptions are just as important as reality, and twelve years of divided control during the Reagan and Bush administrations fostered the sense among some Republicans that CBO's institutional loyalty was actually just partisanship. William Safire, OTA's old critic during the 1970s, gave voice to this perception in an essay in *The New York Times* in February 1993, following President Clinton's state-of-the-union address on the economy. Supporting Republican legislators who had scoffed during the speech at Clinton's assertion that CBO is politically neutral, Safire implied that perhaps the agency should be renamed the DCBO, referring to it as the "Democratic Congressional Budget Office."[17]

Yet it was not long into the Clinton administration that CBO's claims of neutrality began to ring true to its erstwhile Republican critics. In February 1994, just a year after the state-of-the-union address, CBO released a report that, in the hands of Republicans, amounted to a major critique of the administration's health care plan. The agency reported that while the plan would likely reduce overall spending and increase insurance coverage, it would dramatically increase the budget deficit. Opponents of the administration seized on the report as evidence of what they had been arguing: that the Clinton plan would create a large, complex, and expensive federal bureau-

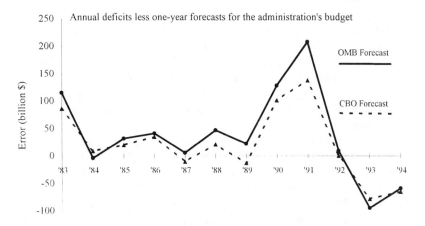

Figure 2. CBO/OMB Deficit Forecasting Error
Source: Congressional Budget Office, Office of Management and Budget

cracy to do what should be done in the marketplace.[18] Legislators held three hearings on the CBO study itself, and it became one of the many eventually lethal arrows shot into the Clinton health care plan.

After the election of 1994 gave them majority status, Republicans on the Hill warmed to CBO even more, finding it a useful ally in their "revolution." In one of the early bills to be passed in 1995, the Unfunded Mandates Reform Act, Republicans gave CBO the key role of conducting scoring of the financial effects on states of federal policy. In the Summer of 1995, the Republican appropriation for the legislative branch increased CBO's budget and added twenty-five staff! It is noteworthy that CBO was one of very few agencies in the federal government, and the only congressional agency, to receive a funding increase in the first Republican appropriation in four decades.[19] The same bill that eliminated OTA, held CRS even with the previous year, and trimmed GAO significantly, actually increased CBO's budget by a small margin. By 1995, CBO had established its bipartisan credentials sufficiently to win the most important endorsement of all. Republican enthusiasm for CBO had replaced skepticism in a very short time. CBO was doing nothing differently than it had before—serving as an ally of Congress.

THE GENERAL ACCOUNTING OFFICE

The last of the congressional support agencies, GAO, is the least like OTA. It dwarfs the other agencies in size. Even after a reduction in budget ordered by congressional Republicans, GAO's $443 million appropriation is five times larger than those of CRS and CBO combined. GAO has a well-institutionalized system of hierarchical control, and detailed, standardized operating procedures that make it far more bureaucratic than was OTA or the other congressional agencies. Mosher describes GAO as "essentially an administrative organization" that "probably approaches the Weberian model of a bureaucracy as closely as most other administrative organizations."[20] This organizational form could not be much more different from OTA's lean, flat, and collegial structure.

But the most important difference from OTA stems from GAO's oversight and accounting function. As the Commission on the Operation of the Senate wrote in 1976, GAO's accounting and oversight role contrasts sharply with that of the other three congressional agencies.[21] This role has not always been well defined, and GAO's place in the system of separation of powers has been the subject of protracted debate. Unlike OTA, CRS, and CBO, the original GAO was not a congressional support agency. Its origins are executive in nature. The Budget and Accounting Act of 1921 created GAO out of an accounting office in the Treasury Department, and GAO's initial 1700 employees transferred from the Treasury. The Budget Act indicated that GAO was to be independent of the executive branch, but did not clearly state that it was to be a congressional agency. The act, which also created the Bureau of the Budget, specified that GAO was to be "independent of the executive departments and under the control and direction of the Comptroller General."[22] It transferred all property, documents, furniture, and staff from the Office of the Comptroller of the Treasury to the new GAO, which was to have authority to settle and adjust all claims by or against the United States.

Throughout its first decades, GAO struggled to maintain its independence from the executive branch, without much regard for its thin connections to Congress. Attempts were made to move part or all of GAO back into the Treasury under Presidents Harding and Hoover, and Roosevelt's Brownlow Committee also recommended that some of GAO's functions be returned to the executive branch.

Not until the Reorganization Act of 1945 was GAO defined as part of the legislative branch, but attempts to shift part of the agency back to the executive still continued. In 1949, the first Hoover Commission recommended that primary government accounting functions being performed by GAO be transferred to the Treasury, and in 1950 Congress finally made a transfer of those functions. Most accounting and financial reporting was shifted to executive agencies, leaving GAO with the monitoring and standard-setting functions for which it is now known.

Even that apparent resolution to the nearly thirty-year-old problem of how independent GAO was to be from the executive branch did not settle the question of whether the agency was truly congressional in character. By 1966, a decade after being defined as a congressional agency, only eight percent of GAO's work was performed at the request of Congress.[23] GAO functioned essentially as an independent agency autonomous from both branches.

Elmer Staats, who was appointed Comptroller General and head of GAO in 1967, began a period of transition that finally saw GAO grow markedly closer to the legislature. Staats emphasized congressional service at the agency, expanded staff to include specialists with backgrounds other than accounting, and moved GAO into the business of program evaluation. Prior to Staats's arrival, "accounting" at GAO had been defined in the traditional sense of evaluating efficiency and financial procedure. By the late 1960s, GAO's brand of accounting increasingly included the assessment of policy results—potentially a far more politically contentious undertaking.

The Legislative Reorganization Act of 1970, which expanded GAO, endorsed the new activity, directing GAO to undertake outcome evaluations and cost-benefit analyses—either at congressional request or on its own initiative. By the early 1970s, GAO was firmly established in the business of policy evaluation. In many ways, this new role marked only the beginning of GAO's status as a congressional support agency. By 1976, congressional requests still made up only 35 percent of GAO's work, while the other three congressional agencies were dedicated entirely to servicing requests from Congress. The Commission on the Operation of the Senate noted in 1976 that the Comptroller General was not interested in increasing the fraction of work performed for Congress, because he worried about an "imbalance" of too much congressional work, which might jeopardize GAO's "ability to discharge its other responsibilities adequately."[24]

The sense that the agency has "other responsibilities" aside from those specifically directed by Congress has not entirely faded at GAO. In 1984, Mosher observed that some officers at GAO "object vociferously" when GAO is described as a congressional support agency. About 80 percent of the agency's work is now associated with congressional requests, although in some instances GAO solicits the requests. One of GAO's top officers remarked in an interview with the author that "as a service organization we realize we're not *always* going to be the master of what we do" [emphasis added], suggesting that GAO still has the sense that a portion of its work should be independent of mastery or control by legislators.[25] In its annual report, GAO notes that its mission is to serve the public interest by providing both "members of Congress and others who make policy" with analysis and information.[26]

This attitude at GAO is the remnant of its tradition as an independent agency with little or no relationship to the legislature. Congressional demands for responsiveness draw GAO continually closer, as the increasing portion of work performed for Congress shows, but its culture and organization make it slow to respond. GAO's large size also renders it less immediately responsive to congressional demands. The fact that a significant number of its staff work in regional offices across the United States or overseas, for instance, gives it a form of insulation from Congress that the other support agencies do not have. Most staff at GAO do not have regular contacts with Congress, and, on the contrary, often interact more with the executive agencies and programs they monitor and evaluate.

Moreover, GAO has certain independent powers that have been delegated to it by Congress, which it can exercise quite autonomously. The Comptroller General can make legally binding judgments about the legality of certain payments, can decide appeals by losing bidders regarding the potential violation of contracting laws, and has the authority to approve agency accounting systems. This independent authority, combined with a good deal of insulation with respect to internal administrative matters, makes GAO much different from the other three congressional agencies, whose activities are limited to the provision of information, reports, and advisory judgments to Congress.

Despite these differences, GAO has a position of publicly stated neutrality like CRS, CBO, and OTA. Like its smaller sibling agencies, GAO advertises itself as "a non-partisan agency" that provides "accurate information, unbiased analysis, and objective recommendations."[27] At the top of the list of "traditional values of GAO auditing" are "non-partisan, unbiased" work, and "provable facts, uncolored by ideology, preference, or parochialism."[28]

Ironically, GAO's tradition of independence and autonomy have actually worked against the achievement of non-partisanship. In the decades prior to the 1970s and early 1980s, GAO was indeed viewed as a highly credible, non-partisan organization serving no particular political interest. But beginning in the late 1980s, GAO increasingly found itself the subject of charges of bias and criticism stemming from its policy pronouncements. Currently, GAO is viewed by most legislators as the least non-partisan of the three congressional agencies.

The reasons for GAO's difficulty in maintaining its traditional non-partisanship are subtle. Since Elmer Staats's tenure as Comptroller General and the Legislative Reorganization Act of 1970, GAO has been drawn increasingly closer to the legislative process, responding to a growing portion of congressional requests. GAO has brought to this process its long and well-established tradition of making audit-related recommendations, a tradition dating from its independent period. This makes GAO the only congressional agency that officially offers policy recommendations. This tradition has increasingly placed GAO in the position of promoting the positions of individual legislators and committees.

The result has been predictable: criticism from legislators who object to its recommendations. In the 1980s and early 1990s, criticisms came chiefly from Republicans, who resented the greater use made of GAO by majority Democrats, especially committee chairs. But Democrats also voiced unhappiness with GAO when the agency stepped on guarded turf or surprised them with unexpected reports. For example, a series of reports in 1988–1990 on western land use in the United States angered many Democrats from western states, such as Senator Harry Reid of Nevada, chair of the Legislative Branch Subcommittee in the Senate, because it recommended increased grazing fees and higher charges for access to mineral resources.

GAO's tradition of independence, and its desire to be more the "master of what we do," has made it very slow to develop the kinds of mechanisms in place at OTA, CRS, and CBO for developing political neutrality. GAO's size and the momentum of a long history of quasi-autonomy from both Congress and the executive have made it less nimble at responding to the demands of serving many masters equally than was OTA. For example, GAO angered Senator Robert Byrd when he was chair of the Appropriations Committee with its study of the line-item veto, because it failed to consult with him before releasing the report—a basic and easily avoided mistake that would not have been made at OTA, CRS, or CBO.

The demands for fairness, equal access, and balanced responsiveness are placing strong pressures on GAO. The agency barely survived several attempts to severely reduce its budget in the early 1990s. In 1992, the Comptroller General promised the reform of at least one GAO practice that led to charges of partisanship, the detailing of agency staff to work for committee chairs. Even before the change in control in 1995, GAO was experiencing strong equilibrating pressures similar to those felt by OTA and CBO in the 1970s, despite its lethargic response. In 1995, the bill that eliminated OTA imposed the first in a two-year set of budget reductions aimed at shrinking GAO by 25 percent, and the attendant restructuring is likely to give impetus to GAO's growing responsiveness to congressional needs. So, like CRS and CBO, GAO operates its own version of the strategy of neutrality that was a hallmark of OTA. GAO's development of the strategy has been slow and imperfect compared to that of the other agencies, but is unmistakably evident.

Chapter 9

Conclusion

CRS, CBO, and GAO emerged from conditions different than those of OTA, but they have responded to a similar set of incentives regarding politicization. This fact tends to support the finding that OTA's strategy of neutrality was not the result of circumstances unique to that agency, but indeed reflects a general phenomenon. With that idea in mind, it is worthwhile standing back and posing two concluding questions about the record of OTA's strategy of neutrality and the agency's rise and fall in Congress. First, how should this agency be judged as a political organization? And second, what lessons does its experience offer as a case study in the politics of expertise?

JUDGING OTA

By the crudest measure—its ability to sustain itself—OTA was ultimately a failure as an organization. If one views the first imperative of any bureaucratic actor as ensuring its own survival, then OTA eventually failed to measure up. But the agency should also be judged against other measures, such as the technical quality of its expertise, and the effect of its work on policy. On the first of these measures, OTA can only be judged a success. For at least its final decade, the agency's work earned nearly uniformly high marks for technical competence and soundness. Staff, members, and a wide range of policy experts outside Congress accorded OTA praise for the quality of the expertise reflected in its work.[1] The efforts at imitation by European legislatures were perhaps the highest form of this praise. That it could develop such a reputation in such a short period, and after such ignominious beginnings, is noteable.

As for its effect on policy, OTA's performance was mixed. It was probably as successful at influencing external policy analysis activities as the internals of the legislative process. Its studies often established themselves as central elements of the scholarly literature on various policy problems, making OTA one of the flagship performers of policy analysis in the country, and perhaps the definitive assessor of the social impacts of technology. It was sometimes said in the field that "technology assessment is whatever OTA is doing at the moment." For this reason, the agency developed a relatively large informal following outside Congress among scholars.

But OTA's impact on congressional politics was insufficient to save it from the budget axe. Indeed it rarely made a major mark on the legislative process. It did not swing votes or change public opinion in a visible way, but typically labored in comparatively obscure fields—helping committees frame issues and construct the policy agenda. There is power in that process to be sure, and OTA influenced policy by contributing in that way. One can count many major bills and dozens of minor ones that bear OTA's mark, from SDI appropriations to the Brady Bill. But one must peer through a strong microscope to see a direct connection between the agency's research and the outcome of most public policies. One might have asked more of OTA in this regard, as did Senator Mack in 1995. Yet it would have been difficult for the agency to have made a more visible contribution, given the nature of the policy process itself and limits on the degree to which any experts can influence what are at root political decisions.

In the months after the votes that terminated the agency, there was a great deal of speculation among employees and observers of the agency about "what went wrong" and what might have been done differently. Clearly the strategy of neutrality had been functional for survival, but it was not sufficient under the new circumstances. After the election of 1994, this strategy's inadequacy became more clear, but the agency hardly had time to adapt. The neutrality that it had worked so hard to achieve was still an asset. But the cautiousness about promoting itself that had been useful for so long left it vulnerable in a time of budget cuts and staff reductions.

The strategy of neutrality had evolved in a period when Congress' own budget was relatively secure and its internal organization was stable; the chief threats to the agency were associated with favoritism. As a consequence, Gibbons and OTA's board never undertook a strategy of growth in budget and staffing or of expansion in the market for its expertise beyond the committees. OTA's Director of Congressional Relations, Jim Jensen, observed that as a result of the partisan squabbles and jurisdictional struggles of the 1970s and 80s, OTA's mode of operation was "cautious and conservative."² The agency focused on satisfying a limited clientele of committee chairs and ranking minority members, to the exclusion of attempts to build the absolute size of its own constituency.

OTA's authorizing legislation limited the primary market for the agency's studies to the full committees so it was prevented from GAO-like service to all legislators. But OTA might have committed more resources to building a better secondary market in the rest of Congress, by taking greater advantage of studies conducted for committees to provide derivative services to the rest of Congress. Greater efforts by agency employees to form relationships with personal staffs—in addition to committee staffs—and to find ways to help members with their electoral interests would have contributed to the agency's institutionalization. So would a larger press operation to publicize its work in the media and build public awareness of the agency's utility. But in the environment in which OTA operated in the 1980s and early 1990s, that kind of entrepreneurship on the part of the agency was less well rewarded than an emphasis on de-politicization.

A fact that advocates of greater use of policy analysis and technical methods in politics may find disturbing is that until the upheaval of 1995, OTA was rarely criticized for being irrelevant; it was more often attacked for being too relevant to particular political interests. Its strategy of neutrality was not a strategy designed to maximize the legislative impact of expertise in any given episode of policy-making; it was a strategy designed to ensure survival in a particular kind of environment. OTA committed more effort to avoiding making enemies than it did to winning new friends and influencing policy. 1995 brought an entirely new set of circumstances, in which survival was not simply a function of avoiding enemies, but also of relying on friends to justify one's existence. OTA's allies—like Republicans Amo Houghton and Orrin Hatch—had indeed supported it, but they were too few in number to prevail against the budget-cutting tide.

THE POLITICS OF EXPERTISE

What does OTA's evolution tell us about the politics of expertise? Three main lessons stand out. The first concerns the purposes to which legislators put policy expertise. What legislators wanted from OTA might be called political propriety. Individually, they wanted expertise that was responsive and relevant, that was framed in ways that illuminated links between technical claims and political interests. But political propriety also involved a counterintuitive demand, namely that expertise do a legislator no harm. Legislators were frequently more animated by the possibility that expertise from the agency might harm them—usually by undermining an interest or contributing to the cause of a rival—than by the possibility that it help them directly. Above all, legislators asked that agency expertise not damage their positions, that it not surprise or embarrass them. This aspect of political propriety is an adaptation of the Hippocratic standard in medicine: first, information must do no harm.

This political propriety illustrates limits on the influence of experts that would most likely have been comforting to Jefferson in his contemplation of the problem of an uninformed public. If OTA's experience is any guide, circumstances under which legislators make political choices chiefly on the basis of expert claims are indeed rare. Legislators did not cast votes because OTA instructed them what was best; rather, they employed OTA's expertise to sift among problems and frame potential solutions. They then made political judgments—as they are elected to do.

OTA's record also shows that it can be difficult to separate institutional imperatives from policy goals in the use of expertise. Demands for expertise from OTA were tied to the capacity of that expertise to contribute to the power to make policy. Not just at OTA, but at CRS, GAO, and CBO, legislators solicit expertise not simply in pursuit of good policy, but because they want control over the policy process. Policy experts who fail to see that their expertise can serve these two purposes at once may miss an important part of their own role in politics. Knowledge can contribute not just to policy, but indeed to power, and it is likely to be sought more for the latter reason than for the former. In the politics of expertise, the contribution of information to the power to make policy is no less important than its contribution to the content of policy.

A second lesson concerns the way that policy expertise is conveyed from experts to legislators. Academically trained experts are often focused on the presentation of written claims. But at OTA, expertise was often conveyed in the context of personal relationships rather than published words. A large part of OTA's success derived from relationships between individuals on its staff and committee staff. It is less an exaggeration than one might think to say that OTA's role in Congress would not have been diminished had the agency never published a written report. Often, the release of written OTA studies was a symbolic event in the midst of a long personal interaction between employees of the agency and Congress.

The oral tradition of communication is strong in Congress—more so than in many places in the executive branch—and this tradition demands face-to-face contacts between experts and politicians. Remarkably to those steeped in traditional administrative bureaucracy, the value of the spoken word in Congress is often much greater than that of the written phrase. As an aide to a senior Senator told me during my research, in Congress what matters most is what people say, not what they write. To a degree that some scholars trained in the preparation of papers and books might find discomfiting, this rule can apply to experts as well as to politicians.

The third lesson suggested by OTA's record is the most important, and it concerns the normatively attractive goal of eliciting depoliticized advice from experts. A central problem—arguably *the* central problem—in discussions of experts in the policy process concerns politicization. A goal of many advocates of well-informed public policy is ensuring the "neutrality" and credibility of the experts who contribute to politics. We want policy-makers to have available to them the best available knowledge, not merely the tendentious claims or even the "junk science" of those with a stake in outcomes.

But study of the nature of expertise, especially that dealing with disputes among experts, has established that as individuals, experts are rarely objective providers of truth. Experts do not necessarily supply information and analysis that is free of normative judgments. The "facts" and understanding that experts provide are often not easily dissociated from underlying values. At many points along the continuum of scientific and technical discovery or learning are opportunities for experts to exercise discretion that is not strictly objective or "scientific" in nature: in the choice and framing of questions, the adoption of theoretical or empirical models, the interpretation of sometimes ambiguous data, and in the phrasing and presentation of results. Disagreements and claims that are at variance from one another do not necessarily represent a lack of either skill or integrity on the part of experts. Science is capable of posing more questions than it is capable of answering.[3] A large body of problems has the characteristic that they can be framed in scientific terms but are beyond the reach of current empirical or theoretical science to solve. The political problems for which politicians seek information from experts often have these characteristics.

The lesson from OTA's experience is that it is indeed possible for political institutions to elicit the production of neutral-tending expertise under just such circumstances. The key is how institutional structure aggregates individual politicians' demands for information. The problem is not simply a matter of the professionalism of individual experts or the motives of politicians. It is not the case that experts at OTA had no values, no opinions, no position on policies. What is interesting is that the agency chose not to reveal those positions in its work. It is also not the case that OTA employed a special "science" of policy analysis that somehow separated values from facts. OTA's formula was responsiveness to its institutional environment, not unique analytic methods or the employment of somehow apolitical experts.

In Congress, decentralization of power has made a low degree of politicization on the part of captive experts functional for survival. Congressional agencies like OTA are rewarded for being perceived as depoliticized, and they tend to adopt some form of a strategy of neutrality in response. The degree of politicization at these agencies does vary, as a function of their missions and specific circumstances. CRS has probably been the most successful at accomplishing the appearance of neutrality, followed by OTA and CBO, and finally GAO. But what is more important than comparatively small differences between congressional agencies is their much more significant difference as a group from what would be expected on the basis of much of the literature on the politics of expertise—which comes to us from observation of the executive branch.

It is laudable for the conduct of policy analysis that an institution designed to represent political interests in a pluralistic way tends to represent technical knowledge pluralistically also. Congress will never match the capacity of a hierarchical, administrative bureaucracy to organize and assimilate information on the basis of specialized expertise. Nor would that be its proper role as a representative body. But as a forum for eliciting a multiplicity of expert views that can collectively tend toward objectivity and neutrality, Congress appears especially competent, its jettisoning of OTA notwithstanding. Its capacity in this regard complements the tendency of the executive branch to provide expert information in support of more narrowly defined political objectives—expert competence that is more "responsive" than neutral.

So Congress is not as hostile an environment for expertise as is sometimes thought. The conventional wisdom about Congress' lack of receptivity to policy expertise is quite incomplete. It overlooks an important way in which the legislature is actually very effective as a consumer of expertise. This is no small feat in light of the inextricable links between scientific claims and political values. Given that the distinction between the two is so often impossible to draw cleanly, the best that one may hope for is that policy-makers have available to them the honest representation of all expert views. Perhaps the most positive conclusion one can draw from OTA's relatively short relationship with Congress is that captive organizations of experts can provide depoliticized expertise—if institutional arrangements reward it.

What lies ahead for policy expertise in Congress? Without OTA, legislators will increase their reliance on experts with a stake in outcomes. Recentralization of power in the House in the 104th Congress suggests a decrease in the impetus for neutral expertise from the congressional agencies. The autonomy of committee chairs has been curtailed in favor of the authority of the Speaker, and to a degree not seen in years, the direction of policy has begun to be set by party leaders. These changes diminish the incentives for inclusiveness that OTA experienced. And to the extent that the majority party is able to exclude the minority from agenda-setting and policy formulation, the impetus for support agencies to include the perspectives of both parties may decline also.

It is tempting to incorporate the abolition of OTA into my account of power and expertise, since the event happened just as the House went through its first significant re-centralization of power in decades. Indeed, OTA was discarded at the same time that the House leadership strengthened its ties with partisan providers of expertise like the Heritage Foundation.

My account does suggest that the shift in the organization of power in Congress should produce a shift in the strategies of experts. Like OMB in the White House, congressional policy experts should grow more politicized, or, like PSAC, they should be abandoned. OTA's demise is consistent with this expectation, but it would overstate the case to say the agency was terminated because Republicans wanted only partisan advice. OTA's termination was a result of its vulnerability in times of cost-cutting, and was not simply the product of a re-centralized House. Had it survived, and should the change in the organization of power persist, then one might have been able to observe a shift away from its strategy of neutrality in response to that re-centralization.

If the Republican party does consolidate its power in future elections, and the structural trends inside Congress begun 1995 continue, we should indeed expect to see the other expert agencies in Congress beginning to move away from their long-standing strategies of neutrality.

There are several factors that will tend to militate against such a shift in the near future, though. In an era when party unity is extraordinarily difficult to maintain in Congress, it is likely that the parochial interests of legislators will work against centralized Republican control over information. The stubbornly decentralized Senate is also likely to remain a place that rewards inclusiveness by its experts. And continued voter dissatisfaction with both parties suggests increasingly significant third-party activity and the possibility that neither Republicans nor Democrats will succeed at maintaining control of Congress for very long. Under such circumstances, incentives for congressional experts to redouble their efforts at non-partisanship would exist. Whatever outcomes electoral forces produce, the future of institutionalized policy expertise in the legislature should continue to follow trends in the organization of power.

NOTES

PREFACE

1. Thomas Jefferson, Letter to William Charles Jarvis, Sep. 28, 1820, in *The Writings of Thomas Jefferson*, Memorial Edition, Vol. XV (Washington, D.C.: The Thomas Jefferson Memorial Association of the United States, 1904), National Archives, Washington, D.C.

CHAPTER 1. KNOWLEDGE AND POWER

1. James Allen Smith, *Brookings at Seventy-Five* (Washington, D.C.: Brookings Institution, 1991).

2. Sheila Jasanoff, *The Fifth Branch: Science Advisors as Policymakers* (Cambridge, Mass.: Harvard University Press, 1990).

3. Figure based on the number of registered political action committees between 1974, when explosive growth began, and the early 1990s, when growth leveled out. See Norman Ornstein, Thomas E. Mann, and Michael J. Malbin, *Vital Statistics on Congress 1993–1994* (Washington, D.C.: Congressional Quarterly, Inc., 1994).

4. Christopher Hill, "The Future of the Congressional Support Agencies," testimony before the Subcommittee on Legislative [sic], Committee on Appropriations, U.S. House of Representatives, and the Subcommittee on the Legislative Branch, Committee on Appropriations, U.S. Senate, 104th Congress, Feb. 2, 1995.

5. Ornstein, Mann, and Malbin, *Vital Statistics on Congress 1993–1994*.

6. John Kingdon, *Agendas, Alternatives, and Public Policies*, 2nd ed. (New York: Little, Brown, 1995).

7. For this view, see: Carol Weiss, "Congressional Committees as Users of Analysis," *Journal of Policy Analysis and Management*, 8(3) (1989): pp. 411–431; Charles O. Jones, "Why Congress Can't Do Policy Analysis (or words to that ef-

fect)," *Policy Analysis* 2(2)(1976): pp. 251–264; Allen Schick, "The Supply and Demand for Analysis on Capitol Hill," *Policy Analysis* 2(2) (1976): pp. 215–234; Edward Schneier, "The Intelligence of Congress: Information and Public Policy Patterns," *The Annals of the American Academy of Political and Social Science* (388) (1970).

8. Thomas E. Mann, ed., *A Question of Balance* (Washington, D.C.: Brookings Institution, 1990).

9. James C. Wright, Jr., "The View from Capitol Hill," in William H. Robinson and Clay H. Wellborn, *Knowledge, Power and the Congress*(Washington, D.C.: Congressional Quarterly Books, 1991).

10. Michael Barone and Grant Ujifusa, *The Almanac of American Politics 1988* (Washington, D.C.: National Journal, 1987), p. 483.

11. Lee Metcalf, Statement in *The Congressional Record*, 93rd Congress, 2nd session, March 19, 1974, p. S3844.

12. Richard Fenno, *Congressmen in Committees* (Boston: Little, Brown & Company, 1973).

13. Charles E. Lindblom, *The Policy-Making Process* (Englewood Cliffs, N.J.: Prentice-Hall, 1968).

14. For instance, see: David Whiteman, "The Fate of Policy Analysis in Congressional Decision Making: Three Types of Use in Committees," *Western Political Quarterly* 38(2) (Jun. 1985); Janice M. Beyer and Harrison M. Trice, "The Utilization Process: A Conceptual Framework and Synthesis of Empirical Findings," *Administrative Science Quarterly* 27 (Dec. 1982): pp. 591–622; Nathan Caplan, Andrea Morrison, and R. Stambaugh, *The Use of Social Science Knowledge in Policy Decisions at the National Level* (Ann Arbor: Institute for Social Research, 1975).

15. James M. Rogers, *The Impact of Policy Analysis* (Pittsburgh: University of Pittsburgh Press, 1988).

16. Throughout, I use the term "expertise" to refer to policy expertise: scientific or technical skills, judgment, and knowledge applied to the substance of policy problems. Policy analysts, economists, engineers, social and physical scientists, and others bring policy expertise to politics. I distinguish policy expertise from political expertise, such as that provided by campaign managers, pollsters, media advisors, or legislative strategists.

17. For statements of this view, see: Daniel E. Ponder, "Reformulating Neutral Competence Theory: Expertise and Responsiveness in the Carter Administration," Paper Prepared for Delivery at the Annual Meeting of the American Political Science Association, New York, Sept. 1–4, 1994; Francis E. Rourke, "Responsiveness and Neutral Competence in American Bureaucracy," *Public Administration Review* 52(6) (Nov./Dec. 1992): pp. 539–546; Terry M. Moe, "The Politicized Presidency," in John E. Chubb and Paul E. Peterson, eds., *The New Direction in American Politics* (Washington, D.C.: Brookings Institution, 1985); Hugh Heclo, "OMB and the Presidency—the problem of 'neutral competence,'" *The Public Interest* 38 (Winter 1975): pp. 80–98; Herbert Kaufman, "Emerging Conflicts in the Doctrines of Public Administration," *American Political Science Review* 50 (Dec. 1956): pp. 1057–1073.

18. The issue of CBO's loyalties is taken up in Chapter 8.

19. Analysts of science and technology policy have traditionally made a distinction between two modes of interaction between scientific experts and policy makers. This distinction was originally suggested by Brooks: "policy for science," namely policy directed at the funding, administration, and oversight of science, and "science in policy," namely the use of scientific expertise in the making of policy more generally. See Harvey Brooks, "The Scientific Advisor," in Robert Gilpin and Christopher Wright, eds., *Scientists and National Policy-Making* (New York: Columbia University Press, 1964). In this traditional terminology, a sharp distinction between "science" and "technology" is often not drawn. OTA's work is chiefly addressed to the latter of Brooks's forms of policy.

CHAPTER 2. A THEORY OF THE POLITICIZATION OF EXPERTISE

1. See Robert K. Merton, "The Normative Structure of Science," in *The Sociology of Science: Theoretical and Empirical Investigations* (Chicago: University of Chicago Press, 1973); and Michael Polanyi, "The Republic of Science," *Minerva* 1 (1962): pp. 54–73.

2. For reviews, see: Jasanoff, *The Fifth Branch*; and Sheila Jasanoff, *et al.*, eds. *Handbook of Science, Technology and Society* (Beverly Hills: Sage Publications, 1994), pp. 554–571.

3. Franklin D. Roosevelt, Letter to Vannevar Bush, Director of the Office of Scientific Research and Development, November 17, 1944, in Vannevar Bush, *Science: The Endless Frontier, A Report to the President on a Program for Postwar Scientific Research*, July 1945 (reprinted, Washington, D.C.: National Science Foundation, 1960), p. 3.

4. *The Brookings Institution 1994 Annual Report* (Washington, D.C.: The Brookings Institution, 1994); *Facts about RAND* (Santa Monica: RAND, 1994).

5. *Institute for Policy Studies 30th Anniversary Report* (Washington, D.C.: Institute for Policy Studies, 1993); *The Heritage Foundation 1993 Annual Report* (Washington, D.C.: The Heritage Foundation, 1993); *AEI Annual Report* (Washington, D.C.: American Enterprise Institute, 1994); *Cato Institute Annual Report* (Washington, D.C.: The Cato Institute, 1993).

6. Kaufman, "Emerging Conflicts in the Doctrines of Public Administration."

7. Ponder, "Reformulating Neutral Competence Theory: Expertise and Responsiveness in the Carter Administration"; Rourke, "Responsiveness and Neutral Competence in American Bureaucracy"; Moe, "The Politicized Presidency."

8. Heclo, "OMB and the Presidency—the problem of 'neutral competence,'" p. 81.

9. *Ibid.*

10. Moe, "The Politicized Presidency."

11. Rourke argues that there is a distinction between the perspective of Democratic and Republican presidents. Because Republicans have tended to perceive the bureaucracy as inherently liberal in orientation, they have seen the promotion of

responsive competence as a means for correcting political bias. Democrats, on the other hand, have tended to view the bureaucracy as too fragmented and passive for effective action, and so have seen the promotion of responsive competence as a means for gaining control of unresponsive—rather than biased—institutions. Rourke, "Responsiveness and Neutral Competence in American Bureaucracy," p. 540.

12. Moe, "The Politicized Presidency."

13. *Ibid.*, p. 427.

14. Heclo, "OMB and the Presidency—the problem of 'neutral competence,'" p. 83.

15. Moe, "The Politicized Presidency."

16. *Ibid.*

17. The terms "neutral competence" and "responsive competence," which are sometimes used to describe the politicization of experts and administrators, can be ambiguous. They suggest that a sharp distinction exists between the two; in fact, it is impossible to designate an event or time at which OMB was converted from a wholly neutral to a wholly responsive organization. For this reason, it is preferable to refer to degrees of politicization and the direction of organizational evolution rather than assigning organizations to binary categories.

18. George B. Kistiakowsky, *A Scientist at the White House: The Private Diary of President Eisenhower's Special Assistant for Science and Technology* (Cambridge, Mass.: Harvard University Press, 1976). For more on the history of PSAC and its related offices see: Gregg Herken, *Cardinal Choices: Presidential Science Advising from the Atomic Bomb to SDI* (New York: Oxford University Press, 1992); Wolfgang Panofsky, "The Presidency and Science Advising: The PSAC Model," in Kenneth W. Thompson, ed. *The Presidency and Science Advising*, Vol. III (New York: University Press of America, 1990); Bruce L.R. Smith, *U.S. Science Policy Since World War II* (Washington, D.C.: Brookings Institution, 1990); Alvin Weinberg, "Topics and Questions in Science Advising," in Thompson, *The Presidency and Science Advising*; and House of Representatives, Committee on Science and Technology, *A History of Science Policy in the United States, 1940–1985*, Science Policy Study Background Report No. 1, 99th Congress, 2nd Session, Sep. 1986.

19. Herken, *Cardinal Choices*; Weinberg, "Topics and Questions in Science Advising"; Kistiakowsky, *A Scientist at the White House.*

20. Herken, *Cardinal Choices*, p. 142.

21. James Killian, *Sputnik, Scientists, and Eisenhower* (Cambridge, Mass.: MIT Press, 1977).

22. Panofsky, "The Presidency and Science Advising: The PSAC Model."

23. Solomon J. Buchsbaum, "Advising Presidents: A Twenty Year Perspective," in Thompson, *Science Advising*, pp. 45–46.

24. PSAC has been followed by a series of EOP offices, both inside and outside the White House itself: the Office of Science and Technology Policy, the White House Science Council, the President's Council of Advisors on Science and Technology, and the National Science and Technology Council. By and large, these offices have functioned quite differently from PSAC. Predictably, these offices have generally been designed to guarantee political loyalty to the administration; none have had

the combination of PSAC's independence and influence—during its early days. These successors to PSAC fit the expectations of neutral competence theory.

CHAPTER 3. OTA: "THE OFFICE OF WHAT?"

1. Emilio Daddario, Interview with the author, Dec. 19, Washington, D.C., 1990.

2. P.L. 92–484. Technology Assessment Act of 1972. U.S. Congress, 92nd Congress, 2nd Session, Oct. 13.

3. Nancy Carson, "Process, Prescience, and Pragmatism: The Office of Technology Assessment," Paper Prepared for the Eleventh Annual Research Conference of the Association of Public Policy Analysis and Management, Nov. 2–4, 1989.

4. Smith, *Science Policy Since World War II.*

5. Again, it should be noted that a clear distinction between science and technology was not always made in these discussions. For instance, the President's "Science" Advisors had been manifestly focused on space and missile technology. One sometimes finds the terms being used interchangeably. In some cases the mixing of words can be misleading, while in others it is probably of little consequence.

6. Precursor to the Congressional Research Service of the Library of Congress.

7. National Academy of Sciences, *Technology: Processes of Assessment and Choice* (Washington, D.C.: National Academy Press, 1968).

8. Jack Brooks, Statement in *The Congressional Record*, Feb. 8, 1972, p. H873, cited in Barry Casper, "The Rhetoric and Reality of Congressional Technology Assessment," in Thomas Kuehn and Alan Porter, eds., *Science, Technology and National Policy* (Ithaca: Cornell University Press, 1981).

9. In the minds of many members of Congress, OTA's board of directors was to function largely as a joint committee, staffed by the OTA employees, and advised by the private council. It took several years before the respective roles of the board, the director, and the council were firmly established. At first council members exercised considerable influence, even developing an agenda of their own for OTA, although there was uncertainty about whether their purpose was to advise the director or the board. Eventually, legislators on the board asserted control over the agency, and the influence of the council waned. At the same time, the board slowly evolved into less of an operating committee, accepting the interests of other members in OTA's work and the fact that an office dedicated to serving all committees could not easily be controlled by such a small group.

10. See testimony at the joint hearing of the Legislative Branch Subcommittees of the House and Senate Appropriations Committees, Feb. 2, 1995, by David M. Mason of the Heritage Foundation and Norman J. Ornstein of the American Enterprise Institute.

11. Fiscal year.

12. Note that many of the House committee names listed here changed in the 104th Congress. Prior to 1995, the Science Committee was the Science, Space, and Technology Committee, the Commerce Committee was the Energy and Commerce

Committee, the International Relations Committee was the Foreign Affairs Committee, and the Government Reform and Administration Committee was the Government Operations Committee.

13. Fortney Stark, Statement in *The Congressional Record*, 103rd Congress, 2nd Session, Apr. 1, 1993, p. H1851.

14. John Tower, Statement in *The Congressional Record*, 95th Congress, 1st Session, Aug. 4, 1977, pp. 26950–26951.

15. Lloyd Bentsen, Statement in *The Congressional Record*, 95th Congress, 2nd Session, Mar. 1, 1978, pp. 5202–5203.

16. For a discussion of rhetorical use of policy analysis, see Giandomenico Majone, *Evidence, Argument, and Persuasion in the Policy Process* (New Haven: Yale University Press, 1989).

17. See Keith Krehbiel, *Information and Legislative Organization* (Ann Arbor: University of Michigan Press, 1991) for illustrations and discussion of information theory in the legislative context.

18. See Rogers, *The Impact of Policy Analysis*, for an overview of this debate. Also see Whiteman, "The Fate of Policy Analysis in Congressional Decision Making," for a discussion of congressional use of several OTA studies in the agency's early years.

19. Chris Jenkins, "The Office of WHAT?," *San Diego Union*, Nov. 24, 1991: p. D–1.

CHAPTER 4. BUILDING OTA: THE SEPARATION OF POWERS

1. Emilio Daddario, Interview with the author, Dec. 19, 1990, Washington, D.C.

2. George Brown, Interview with the author, Mar. 22, 1995, Washington, D.C.

3. Smith, *Science Policy Since World War II*, p. 97.

4. John H. Gibbons, "Technology and Law in the Third Century of the Constitution," in William Golden, ed., *Science and Technology Advice to the President, Congress, and Judiciary* (New York: Pergamon Press, 1988), p. 416.

5. For literature on these subjects referring to OTA's establishment, see: Michael Mezey, "The Legislature, the Executive, and Public Policy: the Futile Quest for Congressional Power," in James A. Thurber, *Divided Democracy: Cooperation and Conflict Between the President and Congress* (Washington, DC: Congressional Quarterly Press, 1991), pp. 99–122; James P. Pfiffner, "Divided Government and the Problems of Government," in Thurber, *Divided Democracy,* pp. 39–60; Louis Fisher, *The Politics of Shared Power: Congress and the Executive,* 2nd ed. (Washington, D.C.: Congressional Quarterly Press, 1987); James Sundquist, *The Decline and Resurgence of Congress* (Washington, D.C.: The Brookings Institution, 1981); James A. Thurber, "Policy Analysis on Capitol Hill: Issues Facing the Four Analytic Support Agencies of Congress," *Policy Sciences Journal* 6 (1977): pp. 101–111.

Leroy N. Rieselbach, *Congressional Reform in the Seventies* (Morristown, N.J.: General Learning Press, 1987).

6. Charles Mosher, Statement in *The Congressional Record*, 92nd Congress,

2nd Session, Feb. 8, 1972, p. 3200. The majority of debate and consideration of H.R. 10243 took place in the House. In the Senate, the Rules Committee reported an amended version of the House bill H.R. 10243, and it passed on the floor under a unanimous consent agreement. For the comments of Sen. Kennedy and Sen. Everett Jordan, Chair of the Rules and Administration Committee, see: Senate, Committee on Rules and Administration, Subcommittee on Computer Services, "Technology Assessment for the Congress," Hearing on S.2302 and H.R.10243. 92nd Congress, 2nd Session, Mar. 2, 1972.

7. Olin Teague, Statement in *The Congressional Record*, 92nd Congress, 2nd Session, Feb. 8, 1972, p. 3200.

8. House of Representatives, Committee on Science and Technology, Subcommittee on Science, Research, and Technology, Hearing, 96th Congress, 1st Session, Oct. 10, 1979. Several authors affiliated with the agency have remarked on this point: Carson, "Process, Prescience and Pragmatism"; Gibbons, "Technology and Law in the Third Century of the Constitution"; John H. Gibbons and Holly L. Gwin, "Technology and Governance," *Technology in Society* 7 (1987), pp. 333–352.

9. Lauren H. Holland and Robert A. Hoover, *The MX Decision* (Boulder, Col.: Westview Press, 1985); Mezey, "The Legislature, the Executive, and Public Policy."

10. Morris Udall and Ted Stevens, Letter to OTA Director John Gibbons, May 5, 1980. Congressional Correspondence Files, Office of Technology Assessment, Washington, D.C.

11. Holland and Hoover, *The MX Decision*.

12. Office of Technology Assessment, *Ballistic Missile Defense—Background Paper* (Washington, D.C.: Office of Technology Assessment, 1984). The study was requested by the House Armed Services Committee and the Senate Foreign Relations Committee.

13. According to OTA Director John Gibbons, the Pentagon would not identify any specific data, sentences, or sections that revealed classified information, but argued instead that as a whole the report provided too much useful analysis and information to the Soviet Union. John Gibbons, "How John Gibbons Runs Through Political Minefields: Life at the OTA," Interview with John Gibbons. *Technology Review* (Oct 1988): pp. 47–51.

14. Office of Technology Assessment, *SDI: Technology, Survivability, and Software* (Washington, D.C.: U.S. Government Printing Office, 1988).

15. After 1980, energy studies comprised about a tenth of OTA's output of reports.

16. For more on the administration's handling of the plan, see: James L. Cochrane, "Carter Energy Policy and the Ninety-fifth Congress," in Craufurd D. Goodwin, ed., *Energy Policy in Perspective* (Washington, D.C.: The Brookings Institution, 1981), pp. 547–600; Pietro S. Nivola, *The Politics of Energy Conservation* (Washington, D.C.: Brookings Institution, 1986).

17. James E. Katz, *Congress and National Energy Policy* (New Brunswick, N.J.: Transaction Books, 1984).

18. Katz, *Congress and National Energy Policy*; Cochrane, "Carter Energy Policy and the Ninety-fifth Congress."

19. Vincent J. McBrierty, "Technology Assessment for Parliaments at National and European Level," *Futures* 20 (Feb. 1988): pp. 3–18.

20. Norman Vig, "Parliamentary Technology Assessment in Europe: A Comparative Perspective," in Gary C. Bryner, ed., *Science, Technology, and Politics: Policy Analysis in Congress* (Boulder: Westview, 1992), pp. 209–226; Mcbrierty, "Technology Assessment for Parliaments at National and European Level."

21. Ruud Smits and Jos Leyten, "Key Issues in the Institutionalization of Technology Assessment," *Futures* 20 (Feb. 1988): pp. 19–36.

22. *Ibid.*

23. Dirk Jaeger and Peter Scholz, "Science and Technology in the German Bundestag Examined Through the Committee on Research and Technology," in Uwe Thaysen, Roger H. Davidson, and Robert Gerald Livingston, eds., *The U.S. Congress and the German Bundestag: Comparisons of Democratic Processes* (Boulder: Westview, 1990), pp. 471–492.

24. Vig, "Parliamentary Technology Assessment in Europe."

25. John H. Gibbons, "Technology Policy," Speech Delivered at MIT, April 28, 1988.

26. Congressional Correspondence Files, Office of Technology Assessment, Washington, D.C.

27. Robert Hershey, "Capitol Hill's High-Tech Tutor," *The New York Times*, July 15, 1989.

CHAPTER 5. SAVING OTA: PARTY POLITICS AND THE
STRATEGY OF NEUTRALITY

1. Public Law 92–484.

2. Harvey Brooks, "Issues in High-Level Science Advising," in William Golden, ed., *Science and Technology Advice to the President, Congress and Judiciary* (New York: Pergamon Press, 1988), p. 53.

3. Jude Wanniski, "Teddy Kennedy's 'Shadow Government,'" *The Wall Street Journal*, Mar. 27, 1973: p. 20.

4. *The National Review*, "Teddy at Work," 25 (Apr. 27, 1973): p. 454; also see Deborah Shapley, "OTA Funds are Up Against the (West Front) Wall," *Science* 181 (1973): p. 928.

5. Barton Reppert, "OTA Emerges as Nonpartisan Player: Surviving a Rocky Start, Science Agency Wins Over Most Skeptics," *The Washington Post*, Jan. 5, 1988.

6. Robert D. Hershey, "Capitol Hill's High-Tech Tutor," *The New York Times*, Jul. 15, 1989: p. F1.

7. The Board changed somewhat in its initial period. In January 1973, Senator Clifford Case and Representative Olin Teague replaced Allott and Cabell, respectively. By the time OTA issued its first report in 1974, Representatives Morris Udall and Marvin Esch had replaced James Harvey and Mike McCormack, and Senator Ted Stevens had replaced Peter Dominick. For more on this period, see: Senate, Committee on Rules and Administration, Subcommittee on Computer Services, "Technology Assessment for the Congress," Committee Print. 92nd Congress, 2nd Session, Nov. 1, 1972; House of Representatives, Committee on Science and Technology, "Toward the Endless Frontier: History of the Committee on Science and Technology, 1959–1979,"

Committee Print (Ken Hechler), 96th Congress, 1980; Office of Technology Assessment, Minutes and Transcripts of Technology Assessment Board Meetings, 1973–1987, OTA Congressional and Public Affairs Office, Washington, D.C.

8. For more, see: Office of Technology Assessment, Minutes and Transcripts of Technology Assessment Board Meetings, 1973–1987, OTA Congressional and Public Affairs Office, Washington, D.C.; Carson, "Process, Prescience and Pragmatism"; Casper, "The Rhetoric and Reality of Congressional Technology Assessment."

9. OTA, "Rules of Procedure, Technology Assessment Board," Unpublished paper, Undated, OTA Information Center, Washington D.C.

10. Office of Technology Assessment, Minutes and Transcripts of Technology Assessment Board Meetings, 1973–1987, OTA Congressional and Public Affairs Office, Washington, D.C.

11. Olin Teague, Letter to Emilio Daddario, OTA Director, with accompanying report, Dec. 22, 1976; Office of Technology Assessment, *Annual Report,* Mar. 15, 1977, OTA Information Center, Washington D.C. The House Commission on Information and Facilities released a review of OTA in 1976 criticizing the agency for poor administrative services and lack of organizational control and order, but it soft-pedalled the staffing problem. The commission commented that Rule 12 introduced into OTA a haphazard variety of staff not under central control, but did not link the staffing practice to politicization or conflict of interest on the part of OTA employees. House of Representatives, House Commission on Information and Facilities, *The Office of Technology Assessment: A Study of its Organizational Effectiveness,* 94th Congress, 2nd Session, Jun. 18, 1976.

12. In my December 19, 1990 interview with him, Daddario maintained that he had resigned only because his work was accomplished, and not in light of political problems.

13. Thomas P. Southwick, "Hill Technology Assessment Office Hit by Controversy, Future Role is Questioned," *Congressional Quarterly,* Jun. 18, 1988: pp. 1202–1203.

14. Constance Holden, "OTA: Daddario's Exit Heightens Strife over Kennedy Role," *Science* 197 (1977): pp. 27–28.

15. William Safire, "The Charles River Gang Returns," *The New York Times,* May 26, 1977. The "Charles River Gang" consisted of Senator Kennedy, his staffer Mottur, and Jerome Wiesner of MIT, ex-science advisor to President John Kennedy.

16. Mottur claims that Kennedy's aims were statesmanlike throughout this period, and in fact the Senator had argued in November 1973 that the board should use an outside agency such as the National Science Foundation or the National Academy of Sciences to screen potential OTA employees, recognizing that many of them had "some form of political backing." But Kennedy had backed down in 1973 at the insistence of Senators Hollings and Humphrey. Office of Technology Assessment, Minutes and Transcripts of Technology Assessment Board Meetings, 1973–1987, OTA Congressional and Public Affairs Office, Washington, D.C.; Ellis Mottur, Interviews with the author, Nov. 5, 20, 1990; Mar. 7, 1991, Washington, D.C.

17. Ellis Mottur, Letter to OTA Chairman Edward Kennedy, Jun. 30, 1977, OTA Archives AC #930, Washington, D.C.

18. John Gibbons, Interviews with the author, Dec. 11, 1990 and Mar. 18, 1991, Washington, D.C.

19. *Ibid.*

20. Office of Technology Assessment, Minutes and Transcripts of Technology Assessment Board Meetings, 1973–1987, OTA Congressional and Public Affairs Office, Washington, D.C.

CHAPTER 6. SUSTAINING OTA: COMMITTEE POLITICS AND THE STRATEGY OF NEUTRALITY

1. Bennett Johnston, Letter to Morris K. Udall, OTA Chair. U.S. Senate, Committee on Energy and Natural Resources, Jul. 10, 1987, OTA Correspondence Files, Washington, D.C.

2. Walter B. Jones, Letter to Morris K. Udall, OTA Chair. House of Representatives, Committee on Merchant Marine and Fisheries, Jul. 13, 1987, OTA Correspondence Files, Washington, D.C.

3. Office of Technology Assessment, Minutes and Transcripts of Technology Assessment Board Meetings, 1973–1987, OTA Congressional and Public Affairs Office, Washington, D.C.

4. Ernest F. Hollings and John C. Danforth, Letter to Morris K. Udall, OTA Chair. U.S. Senate, Committee on Commerce, Science and Transportation, July 25, 1988, OTA Correspondence Files, Washington, D.C.

5. Dante B. Fascell and William S. Broomfield, Letter to Morris K. Udall, OTA Chair. U.S. House of Representatives, Committee on Foreign Affairs, Aug. 1, 1988, OTA Correspondence Files, Washington D.C.

6. Walter B. Jones, Letter to Morris K. Udall, OTA Chair. House of Representatives, Committee on Merchant Marine and Fisheries, Aug. 2, 1988, OTA Correspondence Files, Washington D.C.

7. Patrick Leahy and Richard Lugar, Letter to Morris K. Udall, OTA Chair. U.S. Senate, Committee on Agriculture, Nutrition, and Forestry, Aug. 23, 1988, OTA Correspondence Files, Washington, D.C.

8. Peter Sharfman, Telephone interview with the author, Mar. 28, 1991. Also see Gibbons, "How John Gibbons Runs Through Political Mine Fields."

9. American Enterprise Institute and the Brookings Institution, *Renewing Congress, A Second Report* (Washington, D.C.: American Enterprise Institute for Public Policy Research, 1993), pp. 74–75.

10. Gibbons, "How John Gibbons Runs Through Political Minefields," p. 48.

11. Orrin Hatch, Personal letter to the author, Jun. 7, 1995.

CHAPTER 7. ABOLISHING OTA: BUDGET POLITICS IN THE 104TH CONGRESS

1. Cited in Jonathan D. Salant, "More Hill Cutbacks Coming," *Congressional Quarterly Weekly Report*, Jul. 22, 1995: p. 433.

2. Cited in Jonathan D. Salant, "Tightening Congress's Own Belt," *Congressional Quarterly Weekly Report*, May 20, 1995: p. 1379.

3. Joseph R. Wright, "Testimony on Downsizing the Legislative Branch Sup-

port Agencies," Joint House-Senate Legislative Appropriations Subcommittee, 104th Congress, 1st Session, Unpublished version, Feb. 2, 1995.

4. David M. Mason, "Congressional Support Agencies," Testimony before the Joint Hearing of the Legislative Appropriations Subcommittees, 104th Congress, Unpublished version, Feb. 2, 1995.

5. Republican Conference, U.S. Senate, "Conference Resolution," Unpublished version, Dec. 2, 1994.

6. In fiscal year 1995, just over $1.1 billion of Congress' $2.4 billion appropriation went to the following offices: Architect of the Capitol, Botanic Garden, Congressional Budget Office, Congressional Research Service, General Accounting Office, Government Printing Office, Library of Congress, and Office of Technology Assessment.

7. George Brown, Interview with the author, Mar. 22, 1995, Washington, D.C.

8. John D. Dingell, Statement before the House Appropriations Legislative Subcommittee, Feb. 23, 1995, Unpublished version.

9. Michael G. Oxley, Statement before the Subcommittee on the Legislative Branch, Committee on Appropriations, Unpublished version, Feb. 23, 1995.

10. Salant, "More Hill Cutbacks Coming," p. 443.

11. Ernest F. Hollings, Statement before the Subcommittee on the Legislative Branch, Committee on Appropriations, U.S. Senate, Unpublished version, May 26, 1995.

12. Orrin R. Hatch. Statement before the Subcommittee on Legislative Branch Appropriations, U.S. Senate, Unpublished version, May 26, 1995.

13. House of Representatives, Concurrent Resolution on the Budget, H. Con. Res. 67, 104th Congress, 1st Session, May 15, 1995.

14. House of Representatives, Committee on Appropriations, Legislative Branch Appropriations Bill, 1996, House Report 104–141, 104th Congress, 1st Session, Jun. 15, 1995.

15. David Bonior, Statement in *The Congressional Record*, 104th Congress, 1st Session, Jun. 22, 1995, p. H6206.

16. Richard Armey, Statement in *The Congressional Record*, 104th Congress, 1st Session, Jun. 22, 1995, p. H6204.

17. Richard Gephardt, Statement in *The Congressional Record*, 104th Congress, 1st Session, Jun. 22, 1995, p. H6205.

18. David Bonior, Statement in *The Congressional Record*, 104th Congress, 1st Session, Jun. 22, 1995, p. H6206.

19. For the terms of OTA's closure, see House of Representatives, Conference Report to Accompany H.R. 1854, Appropriations for the Legislative Branch for the Fiscal Year Ending September 30, 1996, and for Other Purposes, House Report 104–212, Jul. 28, 1995.

CHAPTER 8. THE OTHER CONGRESSIONAL SUPPORT AGENCIES

1. William H. Robinson, "The Congressional Research Service: Think Tank and Reference Factory," Paper Prepared for the Eleventh Annual Research Confer-

ence of the Association of Public Policy Analysis and Management, Arlington, Va., November 2–4, 1989.

2. *Ibid.*

3. Evelyn Howard, "The Congressional Research Service," CRS Report for Congress, Washington, D.C.: Congressional Research Service, Aug. 14, 1989.

4. Robinson, "The Congressional Research Service," p. 5.

5. Howard, "The Congressional Research Service"; Sundquist, *The Decline and Resurgence of Congress.*

6. Public Law 79–601. Legislative Reorganization Act of 1946, 79th Congress, 2nd Session, Aug. 2, 1946.

7. Robinson, "The Congressional Research Service," p. 26.

8. Gibbons, "Technology Policy."

9. Robinson, "The Congressional Research Service," p. 25.

10. Aaron B. Wildavsky, *The New Politics of the Budgetary Process* (Glenview, Ill.: Scott, Foresman and Company, 1988).

11. Joel Haveman, *Congress and the Budget* (Bloomington, Ind.: Indiana University Press, 1978); Allen Schick, *Congress and Money* (Washington, D.C.: American Enterprise Institute, 1980).

12. Schick, *Congress and Money.*

13. James L. Blum, "The Congressional Budget Office, On the One Hand, On the Other," in Carol H. Weiss, ed., *Organizations for Policy Analysis: Helping Government Think* (Newbury Park, Cal.: Sage, 1992), p. 225.

14. Congressional Budget Office, *A Profile of the Congressional Budget Office* (Washington, D.C.: Congressional Budget Office, Sep., 1990). Note that a literature exists on economic forecasting accuracy. For instance, see: Mark S. Kamlet, David C. Mowery, and Tsai-Tsu Su, "Whom Do You Trust? An Analysis of Executive and Congressional Economic Forecasts," *Journal of Policy Analysis and Management* 6(3) (1987), pp. 365–384.

15. Executive Office of the President, *Budget of the United States Government, Fiscal Year 1990* (Washington, D.C.: Government Printing Office, 1989), pp. 3–16, 17.

16. There are several types of deficit forecast. Deficits are forecast for the short term and long term, and also assume both that the president's budget proposals are enacted and that no changes in policy are made. (Typically, neither assumption is accurate—CBO claims that slightly less than 30 percent of its deficit forecasting error in the 1980s was due to incorrect policy assumptions, 43 percent from incorrect economic assumptions, and a little less than 30 percent from so-called "technical" assumptions. See Congressional Budget Office, *The Economic and Budget Outlook: Fiscal Years 1991–1995* [Washington, D.C.: Congressional Budget Office, Feb., 1993].) The figures presented here describe what is arguably the most important of the various forecasts: the next-year forecast presented by the President in his budget, assuming his policy proposals are enacted, and the re-estimate of those forecasts by CBO. From those figures, actual budget deficit figures have been subtracted to produce the error figures here.

17. William Safire, "The Great Leap Backward," *The New York Times*, Feb. 18, 1993, p. A23.

18. Alissa J. Rubin, "CBO Turns Budget Spotlight on Health-Care Overhaul," *Congressional Quarterly Weekly Report*, Feb. 12, 1994: p. 290.

19. CBO's appropriation for fiscal year 1996 was $24.3 million, compared with $23.1 million the previous year. The increase was intended to cover the costs of scorekeeping under the unfunded mandates legislation.

20. Frederick Mosher, *The GAO: The Quest for Accountability in American Government* (Boulder: Westview, 1979), p. 343.

21. Senate, Commission on the Operation of the Senate, *Congressional Support Agencies: a Compilation of Papers*, 94th Congress, 2nd Session, Dec., 1976, Senate Doc. No. 94–278, Washington, D.C.: Government Printing Office.

22. U.S. Congress, Budget and Accounting Act of 1921, 67th Congress, Session I, Jun. 10, 1921.

23. Mosher, *The GAO*.

24. Senate, Commission on the Operation of the Senate, *Congressional Support Agencies*, p. 35.

25. Anonymous interview with the author, Oct. 20, 1992.

26. General Accounting Office, *Comptroller General's 1991 Annual Report* (Washington, D.C.: General Accounting Office, 1991).

27. General Accounting Office, *Annual Report*.

28. Mosher, *The GAO*, p. 350.

CHAPTER 9. CONCLUSION

1. In addition to sources cited above, see also *Science, Technology and Congress*, Carnegie Commission on Science, Technology and Government, Washington, D.C., Feb. 1994.

2. Jim Jensen, Telephone interview with the author, Aug. 15, 1995.

3. Alvin Weinberg, "Topics and Questions in Science Advising," in Thompson, *The Presidency and Science Advice*, pp. 103–114.

BIBLIOGRAPHY

Note on Sources

A significant part of this research is based on materials that were located in various offices inside OTA, namely administrative documents, transcripts of legislators' discussions at agency board meetings, correspondence files, and memoranda. After the closure of the agency in 1995, those materials were distributed to a number of locations. Some are now available in the National Archives, including materials cited here as originating in the OTA archives. Complete sets of OTA's collected works from 1974 to 1995 are available at the Archives and at the libraries of the University of California at Santa Barbara, George Washington University, and the University of Maryland at College Park. A CD-ROM version is also available from the Government Printing Office. At the time this book went to press, the Office of the Architect of the Capitol was managing the distribution of many OTA materials to various offices inside Congress. For information about obtaining access to OTA records, contact the Archives, the Architect's Office, or the author.

American Enterprise Institute. *Annual Report.* Washington, D.C.: American Enterprise Institute, 1994.

American Enterprise Institute and the Brookings Institution. *Renewing Congress: A Second Report.* Washington, D.C.: American Enterprise Institute for Public Policy Research, 1993.

Armey, Richard. Statement in *The Congressional Record.* 104th Congress, 1st Session, Jun. 22, 1995, pp. H6204ff.

Anderson, John. Statement in *The Congressional Record.* 92nd Congress, 2nd Session, Feb. 8, 1972, pp. 3210ff.

Arnold, R. Douglas. *The Logic of Congressional Action.* New Haven: Yale University Press, 1990.

Barone, Michael and Grant Ujifusa. *The Almanac of American Politics 1988.* Washington, D.C.: National Journal, 1987.

Bentsen, Lloyd. Statement in *The Congressional Record.* 95th Congress, 2nd Session, Mar. 1, 1978, pp. 5202–5203.

Beyer, Janice M. and Harrison M. Trice. "The Utilization Process: A Conceptual Framework and Synthesis of Empirical Findings." *Administrative Science Quarterly* 27 (Dec. 1982), pp. 591–622.

Bimber, Bruce. "Information as a Factor in Congressional Politics." *Legislative Studies Quarterly,* XVI(4) (Nov. 1991), pp. 585–605.

Bimber, Bruce and David Guston. "Politics by the Same Means: Government and Science in the U.S.," in Sheila Jasanoff, *et al,* eds. *Handbook of Science, Technology and Society.* Beverly Hills: Sage Publications, 1994, pp. 554–571.

Blum, James L. "The Congressional Budget Office: On the One Hand, On the Other," in Carol H. Weiss, ed., *Organizations for Policy Analysis: Helping Government Think.* Newbury Park, Cal.: Sage, 1994, pp. 218–235.

Bonior, David. Statement in *The Congressional Record.* 104th Congress, 1st Session, Jun. 21, 1995, p. H6198.

———. Statement in *The Congressional Record.* 104th Congress, 1st Session, Jun. 22, 1995, p. H6206.

Bradley, R. "Motivations in Legislative Information Use." *Legislative Studies Quarterly* V(3) (Aug. 1980), pp. 393–406.

Brookings Institution. *Annual Report.* Washington, D.C.: The Brookings Institution, 1994.

Brooks, Harvey. "Issues in High-Level Science Advising," in William Golden, ed. *Science and Technology Advice to the President, Congress and Judiciary.* New York: Pergamon Press, 1988, pp. 51–64.

———. "The Scientific Advisor," in Robert Gilpin and Christopher Wright. *Scientists and National Policy-Making.* New York: Columbia University Press, 1964, pp. 73–96.

Buchsbaum, Solomon J. "Advising the President: A Twenty Year Perspective," in Kenneth W. Thompson, ed. *The Presidency and Science Advising,* Vol. VII. New York: University Press of America, 1990, pp. 43–60.

Bush, Vannevar. *Science: The Endless Frontier, A Report to the President on a Program for Postwar Scientific Research,* 1945, Reprinted Washington D.C.: National Science Foundation, 1960.

Caplan, Nathan, Andrea Morrison, and R. Stambaugh. *The Use of Social Science Knowledge in Policy Decisions at the National Level.* Ann Arbor: Institute for Social Research, 1975.

Carson, Nancy. "Process, Prescience, and Pragmatism: The Office of Technology Assessment." Paper Prepared for the Eleventh Annual Research Conference of the Association of Public Policy Analysis and Management, Nov. 2–4, 1989.

Casper, Barry. "The Rhetoric and Reality of Congressional Technology Assessment," in Thomas Kuehn and Alan Porter, eds. *Science, Technology and National Policy.* Ithaca: Cornell University Press, 1981, pp. 327–345.

Cato Institute. *Annual Report.* Washington, D.C.: The Cato Institute, 1989.

Chalk, Rosemary. "Public Participation and Technology Assessment: A Survey of the Legislative History of the Office of Technology Assessment." Congressional Research Service multilith 74–166, U.S. Congress. Sep. 14, 1974. OTA Archive AC #86, Washington, D.C.

Cochrane, James L. "Carter Energy Policy and the Ninety-fifth Congress," in Craufurd D. Goodwin, ed. *Energy Policy in Perspective*. Washington, D.C.: Brookings Institution, 1981, pp. 547–600.

Cohen, Richard E. " 'Information gap' plagues attempt to grapple with growing executive strength." *National Journal* 5, Mar. 17, 1973, pp. 379–388.

Congressional Budget Office. *A Profile of the Congressional Budget Office*. Washington, D.C.: Congressional Budget Office, Sep. 1990.

————. *The Economic and Budget Outlook: Fiscal Years 1991–1995*. Washington, D.C.: Congressional Budget Office, Jan. 1990.

Congressional Quarterly. *U.S. Defense Policy*. Washington, D.C.: Congressional Quarterly Press, 1982.

————. *U.S. Defense Policy*. Washington, D.C.: Congressional Quarterly Press, 1978.

Congressional Quarterly Weekly Report. "Gorsuch Contempt Citation." Dec. 4, 1982, p. 2987.

Daddario, Emilio. Speech before Associates Program. UCLA School of Engineering, Jun. 27, 1975. OTA Archive AC #74, Washington, D.C.

de Marchi, Neil. "Energy Policy under Nixon: Mainly Putting Out Fires," in Craufurd D. Goodwin, ed. *Energy Policy in Perspective*. Washington, D.C.: Brookings Institution, 1981, pp. 395–474.

Dingell, John D. Statement before the House Appropriations Legislative Subcommittee. U.S. House of Representatives. Unpublished version. Feb. 23, 1995.

Esch, Marvin. Statement in *The Congressional Record*. 92nd Congress, 2nd Session, Feb. 8, 1972, p.3200.

Executive Office of the President. Budget of the United States Government, Fiscal Year 1990. Washington, D.C.: Government Printing Office, 1989.

Facts about RAND. Santa Monica, Cal.: RAND, 1994.

Fascell, Dante B. and William S. Broomfield. Letter to OTA Chairman Morris K. Udall. House of Representatives, Committee on Foreign Affairs. Aug. 1, 1988. OTA Correspondence Files, Washington D.C.

Feld, Werner J. and John K. Wildgen. *Congress and National Defense*. New York: Praeger, 1985.

Fenno, Richard, Jr. *Congressmen in Committees*. Boston: Little, Brown & Co, 1973.

Fischer, Frank. *Technocracy and the Politics of Expertise*. London: Sage Publications, 1990.

Fisher, Louis. *The Politics of Shared Power: Congress and the Executive*, 2nd ed. Washington, D.C.: Congressional Quarterly Press, 1987.

Formaini, Robert. *The Myth of Scientific Public Policy*, New Brunswick: Transaction Publishers, 1990.

General Accounting Office. Comptroller General's 1991 Annual Report. Washington, D.C.: General Accounting Office, 1991.

Gephardt, Richard. Statement in *The Congressional Record*, 104th Congress, 1st Session, Jun. 22, 1995, p. H6205.

Gergen, David. "Impartial OTA Future Dubious: A Launching Pad for Kennedy?" *Science Digest*, Sep. 1977, pp. 24–65.

Gibbons, John. "How John Gibbons Runs Through Political Minefields: Life at the OTA." Interview with John Gibbons. *Technology Review*, Oct. 1988, pp. 47–51.

Gibbons, John H. "Technology and Law in the Third Century of the Constitution," in William Golden, ed. *Science and Technology Advice to the President, Congress and Judiciary*, New York: Pergamon Press, 1988, pp. 415–419.

———. "Technology Policy." Speech at M.I.T., sponsored by the Program in Science, Technology and Society, Apr. 28, 1988.

Gibbons, John H. and Holly L. Gwin. "Technology and Governance." *Technology in Society* 7, 1986, pp. 333–352.

Guston, David and Bruce Bimber. "Congressional Organization and the Market for Policy Information." Paper Prepared for Delivery at the 1994 Annual Meeting of the American Political Science Association, The New York Hilton, Sep. 1–4, 1994.

Hahn, Walter and Rosemary Chalk. "The Technology Assessment Act of 1972." Congressional Research Service multilith 72–263, 1972. OTA Archive AC #308, Washington, D.C.

Hatch, Orrin R. Statement before the Subcommittee on Legislative Branch Appropriations, U.S. Senate. Unpublished version, May 26, 1995.

Haveman, Joel. *Congress and the Budget*. Bloomington, Ind.: Indiana University Press, 1978.

Hugh Heclo. "OMB and the Presidency—the problem of "neutral competence." *The Public Interest* 38, Winter 1975, pp. 80–98.

Heineman, Robert A., et. al. *The World of the Policy Analsyt: Rationality, Values, and Politics*. Chatham, N.J.: Chatham House, 1990.

Heritage Foundation. *Annual Report*. Washington, D.C.: Heritage Foundation, 1993.

Herken, Gregg. *Cardinal Choices: Presidential Science Advising from the Atomic Bomb to SDI*. New York: Oxford University Press, 1992.

Hershey, Robert D. "Capitol Hill's High-Tech Tutor." *The New York Times*, Jul. 15, 1989, pp. F1ff.

Hill, Christopher T. "The Future of the Congressional Support Agencies." Testimony before the Subcommittee on Legislative [sic], Committee on Appropriations, U.S. House of Representatives, and the Subcommittee on the Legislative Branch, Committee on Appropriations. U.S. House of Representatives and Senate. Unpublished version, Feb. 2, 1995.

Hofferbert, Richard I. *The Reach and Grasp of Policy Analysis*. Tuscaloosa: University of Alabama Press, 1990.

Holden, Constance. "OTA: Daddario's Exit Heightens Strife over Kennedy Role." *Science* 197, Jul. 1, 1977, pp. 27–8.

———. "Conservatives Troubled About Course of OTA." *Science* 203, Feb. 23, 1979, p. 729.

Holland, Lauren H. and Robert A. Hoover. *The MX Decision*. Boulder: Westview Press, 1985.

Hollings, Ernest F. Statement before the Subcommittee on the Legislative Branch, Commitee on Appropriations, U.S. Senate. Unpublished version, May 26, 1995.

Hollings, Ernest F. and John C. Danforth. Letter to OTA Chairman Morris K. Udall. Senate Committee on Commerce, Science and Transportation. Jul. 25, 1988. OTA Correspondence Files, Washington, D.C.

House of Representatives. Conference Report to Accompany H.R. 1854, Appropriations for the Legislative Branch for the Fiscal Year Ending September 30, 1996, and for Other Purposes, House Report 104–212, Jul.28, 1995.

———. Committee on Appropriations. Legislative Branch Appropriations Bill, 1996, House Report 104–141, 104th Congress, 1st Session, Jun. 15, 1995.

———. Concurrent Resolution on the Budget, H. Con. Res. 67, 104th Congress, 1st Session, May 15, 1995.

———. Committee on Science and Technology. *Toward the Endless Frontier: History of the Committee on Science and Technology, 1959–1979.* Committee Print (Ken Hechler), 1980.

———. Committee on Science and Technology. Subcommittee on Science, Research, and Technology. Hearing. 96th Congress, 1st Session, Oct. 10, 1979.

———. Committee on Science and Technology. Subcommittee on Science, Research, and Technology. *Review of the Office of Technology Assessment and its Organic Act.* Committee Print, 1978.

———. House Commission on Information and Facilities. *The Office of Technology Assessment: A Study of its Organizational Effectiveness.* House Doc. No. 94–538. 94th Congress, 2nd Session, Jun. 18, 1976.

———. Committee on Science and Astronautics. *Establishing the Office of Technology Assessment and Amending the National Science Foundation Act of 1950.* House Report 92–469. 92nd Congress, 1st Session, Aug. 16, 1971.

Howard, Evelyn. "The Congressional Research Service." A CRS Report for Congress, Washington, D.C.: Congressional Research Service, Aug. 14, 1989.

Institute for Policy Studies. *30th Annual Report.* 1993. Washington, D.C.: Institute for Policy Studies, 1993.

Jaeger, Dirk, and Peter Scholz. "Science and Technology in the German Bundestag Examined Through the Committee on Research and Technology," in Uwe Thaysen, Roger H. Davidson, and Robert Gerald Livingston, eds. *The U.S. Congress and the German Bundestag: Comparisons of Democratic Processes.* Boulder: Westview, 1990, pp. 471–492.

Jasanoff, Shiela. *The Fifth Branch: Science Advisors as Policymakers.* Cambridge, Mass.: Harvard University Press, 1990.

Jefferson, Thomas. Letter to William Charles Jarvis, Sep. 28, 1820, in *The Writings of Thomas Jefferson, Memorial Edition* Vol. XV. Washington, D.C.: The Thomas Jefferson Memorial Association of the United States, 1904.

Jenkins, Chris. "The Office of WHAT?" *San Diego Union*, Nov. 24, 1991, p. D–1.

Johnston, Bennett. Letter to OTA Chairman Morris K. Udall. Senate, Committee on Energy and Natural Resources, Jul. 10, 1987. OTA Correspondence Files, Washington, D.C.

Jones, Charles O. "Why Congress Can't Do Policy Analysis (or words to that effect)." *Policy Analysis* 2(2) (1976), pp.251–264.

Jones, Walter B. Letter to OTA Chairman Morris K. Udall. House of Representatives, Committee on Merchant Marine and Fisheries, Aug. 2, 1988, OTA Correspondence Files, Washington D.C.

———. Letter to OTA Director Jack Gibbons. House of Representatives, Committee on Merchant Marine and Fisheries. Jul. 13, 1987, OTA Correspondence Files, Washington, D.C.

Kamlet, Mark S., David C. Mowery, and Tsai-Tsu Su. "Whom Do You Trust? An Analysis of Executive and Congressional Economic Forecasts," *Journal of Policy Analysis and Management* 6(3) (1987), pp. 365–384.

Kaufman, Herbert, "Emerging Conflicts in the Doctrines of Public Administration," *American Political Science Review* 50 (Dec. 1956), pp. 1057–1073.

Katz, James E. *Congress and National Energy Policy*, New Brunswick, N.J.: Transaction Books, 1984.

Killian, James. *Sputnik, Scientists, and Eisenhower*. Cambridge, Mass.: MIT Press, 1977.

Kingdon, John W. *Agendas, Alternatives, and Public Policies*, 2nd ed. New York: Little, Brown, 1995.

Kistiakowsky, George B. *A Scientist at the White House: The Private Diary of President Eisenhower's Special Assistant for Science and Technology*. Cambridge, Mass.: Harvard University Press, 1976.

Kuehn, Thomas and Alan Porter, eds. *Science, Technology and National Policy*, Ithaca: Cornell University Press, 1981.

Lambro, Donald. *Fat City: How Washington Wastes Your Taxes*. South Bend, Ind.: Regnery/Gateway, 1980.

Leahy, Patrick and Richard Lugar. Letter to OTA Chairman Morris K. Udall. Senate, Committee on Agriculture, Nutrition, and Forestry, Aug. 23, 1987, OTA Correspondence Files, Washington, D.C.

Lindblom, Charles E. *The Policy-Making Process*, Englewood Cliffs, N.J.: Prentice-Hall, 1968.

Majone, Giandomenico. *Evidence, Argument, & Persuasion in the Policy Process*. New Haven: Yale University Press, 1989.

Mann, Thomas E., ed. *A Question of Balance*. Washington, D.C.: Brookings Institution, 1990.

Mason, David M. "Congressional Support Agencies." Testimony before the Joint Hearing of the Legislative Appropriations Subcommitees, U.S. House of Representatives and Senate. Unpublished version, Feb. 2, 1995.

Mayhew, David. *Congress: The Electoral Connection*. New Haven: Yale University Press, 1974.

McBrierty, Vincent J. "Technology Assessment for Parliaments at National and European Level," *Futures* 20 (Feb, 1988), pp.3–18.

Merton, Robert K. "The Normative Structure of Science," in Robert K. Merton, *The Sociology of Science: Theoretical and Empirical Investigations*. Chicago: University of Chicago Press, 1973.

Metcalf, Lee. Statement in *The Congressional Record*, 93rd Congress, 2nd session, Mar. 19, 1974, p. S3844.

Mezey, Michael. "The Legislature, the Executive, and Public Policy: the Futile Quest for Congressional Power," in James A. Thurber, ed. *Divided Democracy: Cooperation and Conflict Between the President and Congress*. Washington, D.C.: Congressional Quarterly Press, 1991, pp. 99–122.

Moe, Terry M. "The New Economics of Organization." *American Journal of Political Science* 28(4) (1984), pp. 739–777.

———. "The Politicized Presidency," in John E. Chubb and Paul E. Peterson, eds. *The New Direction in American Politics*. Washington, D.C.: Brookings Institution, 1985, pp. 235–272.

Mosher, Charles. Statement in *The Congressional Record*, 92nd Congress, 2nd Session, Feb. 8, 1972, p. 3200

Mosher, Frederick C. *A Tale of Two Agencies: A Comparative Analysis of the General Accounting Office and the Office of Management and Budget.* Baton Rouge, Louis.: Louisiana State University Press, 1984.

―――. *The GAO: The Quest for Accountability in American Government.* Boulder, Colo.: Westview, 1979.

Mottur, Ellis. Letter to OTA Chairman Edward Kennedy. Jun. 30, 1977. OTA Archives AC #930, Washington, D.C.

Nacht, Michael A. "Why Nuclear Deterrence Will Not Go Away," in Catherine McArdle Kelleher, Frank J. Kerr, and George H. Quester, *Nuclear Deterrence.* Washington, D.C.: Pergamon-Brassey's International Defense Publishers, 1986.

National Academy of Sciences. *Technology: Processes of Assessment and Choice.* National Academy of Sciences. Washington, D.C.: National Academy Press, 1968.

National Review. "Teddy at Work." 25, Apr. 27, 1974, p. 454.

Nivola, Pietro S. *The Politics of Energy Conservation.* Washington, D.C.: Brookings Institution, 1986.

Ornstein, Norman, Thomas E. Mann, and Michael J. Malbin. *Vital Statistics on Congress.* Washington, D.C.: Congressional Quarterly Press, 1994.

Office of Technology Assessment. *Annual Report to the Congress.* (Annual: 1974–1994). OTA Information Center, Washington D.C.

―――. *Justification of Estimates for the Office of Technology Assessment.* Prepared for the Legislative Branch Subcommittes of the House and Senate Appropriations Committee. (Annual: 1974–1995). OTA Information Center, Washington, D.C.

―――. Minutes and Transcripts of Technology Assessment Board Meetings, 1973–1987. OTA Congressional and Public Affairs Office, Washington, D.C.

―――. *SDI: Technology, Survivability, and Software.* Washington, D.C.: U.S. Government Printing Office, 1988.

―――. *Anti-Satellite Weapons, Countermeasures, and Arms Control.* Washington, D.C.: U.S. Government Printing Office, 1985.

―――. *Ballistic Missile Defense Technologies.* Washington, D.C.: U.S. Government Printing Office, 1985.

―――. *Ballistic Missile Defense in Space–Background Paper.* Washington, D.C.: Office of Technology Assessment, 1984.

―――. *MX Missile Basing.* Washington, D.C.: U.S. Government Printing Office, 1981.

―――. *Analysis of Laws Governing Access Across Federal Lands: Options for Alaska.* Washington, D.C.: U.S. Government Printing Office, 1979.

―――. *The Effects of Nuclear War.* Washington, D.C.: U.S. Government Printing Office, 1979.

―――. *Enhanced Oil Recovery in the U.S.* Washington, D.C.: U.S. Government Printing Office, 1978.

―――. *Establishing a 200–Mile Fisheries Zone.* Washington, D.C.: U.S. Government Printing Office, 1977.

―――. *Drug Bioequivalence.* Washington, D.C.: U.S. Government Printing Office, 1974.

———. *Food Information Systems: Summary and Analysis.* Washington, D.C.: U.S. Government Printing Office, 1974.

———. "Rules of Procedure, Technology Assessment Board." Unpublished document, Undated (1973), OTA Information Center, Washington, D.C.

Oxley, Michael G. Statement before the Subcommittee on the Legislative Branch, Committee on Appropriations. U.S. Senate. Unpublished version, Feb. 23, 1995.

Panofsky, Wolfgang. "The Presidency and Science Advising: The PSAC Model," in Kenneth W. Thompson, ed. *The Presidency and Science Advising* Vol. VII. New York: University Press of America, 1990, pp. 27–42.

Pfiffner, James P. "Divided Government and the Problem of Governance," in James A. Thurber, ed. *Divided Democracy: Cooperation and Conflict Between the President and Congress.* Washington, D.C.: Congressional Quarterly Press, 1991, pp. 39–60.

Polanyi, Michael. "The Republic of Science." *Minerva*, 1 (1962), pp. 54–73.

Ponder, Daniel E. "Reformulating Neutral Competence Theory: Expertise and Responsiveness in the Carter Administration." Paper Prepared for Delivery at the Annual Meeting of the American Political Science Association, The New York Hilton, Sep. 1–4, 1994.

P.L. 79–601. Legislative Reorganization Act of 1946. 79th Congress, 2nd Session, Aug. 2, 1946.

P.L. 92–484. Technology Assessment Act of 1972. 92nd Congress, 2nd Session, Oct. 13, 1972.

Reppert, Barton. "OTA Emerges as Nonpartisan Player: Surviving a Rocky Start, Science Agency Wins Over Most Skeptics." *The Washington Post*, Jan. 5, 1988, pp. A17ff.

Republican Conference. "Conference Resolution." U.S. Senate, Unpublished document, Dec. 2, 1994.

———. "Recommendations of the Working Group on Congressional Reform." U.S. Senate, Unpublished document, Jan. 1995.

Rieselbach, Leroy N. *Congressional Reform in the Seventies.* Morristown, N.J.: General Learning Press, 1977.

Robinson, William H. "The Congressional Research Service: Think Tank and Reference Factory." Paper Prepared for the Eleventh Annual Research Conference of the Association of Public Policy Analysis and Management, Nov. 2–4, 1989.

Rogers, James. M. *The Impact of Policy Analysis.* Pittsburgh, Penn.: University of Pittsburgh Press, 1988.

Rourke, Francis E. "Responsiveness and Neutral Competence in American Bureaucracy." *Public Administration Review* 52(6) (Nov./Dec. 1992), pp. 539–546.

Rubin, Alissa J. "CBO Turns Budget Spotlight on Health-Care Overhaul." *Congressional Quarterly Weekly Report*, Feb. 12, 1994, p. 290.

Safire, William. "The Great Leap Backward." *The New York Times*, Feb. 18, 1993, p. A23.

———. "The Charles River Gang Returns." *The New York Times*, May 26, 1977.

Sabatier, Paul and David Whiteman. "Legislative Decision-Making and Substantive Policy Information: Models of Information Flow." *Legislative Studies Quarterly* X(3) (Aug. 1984), pp.395–421.

Salant, Jonathan D. "More Hill Cutbacks Coming." *Congressional Quarterly Weekly Report*, Feb. 11, 1995, p. 433.

———. "Tightening Congress' Own Belt." *Congressional Quarterly Weekly Report*, May 20, 1995, p. 1379.

Sasser, Jim. Statement during hearings on the budget, U.S. Congress, Senate Budget Committee, Jan. 24, 1990.

Schick, Allen. "The Supply and Demand for Analysis on Capitol Hill." *Policy Analysis* 2(2) (1976), pp. 215–234.

———. *Congress and Money*. Washington, D.C.: American Enterprise Institute, 1980.

Science, Technology and Congress: A Report of The Carnegie Commission on Science, Technology and Government, Washington, D.C., Feb. 1994.

Science News. "Kennedy to Chair TAB; Daddario seen for OTA." *Science News* 103 (Jan. 23, 1973), p. 39.

Schneier, Edward. "The Intelligence of Congress: Information and Public Policy Patterns." *The Annals of the American Academy of Political and Social Science* 388 (1970), pp. 14–24.

Senate. Committee on Governmental Affairs. *The Roles, Mission and Operation of the US General Accounting Office*, Committee Print, S. Prt 103–87, 103rd Congress, 2nd Session, Oct., 1994.

———. Committee on Rules and Administration. *Oversight Hearings on the Office of Technology Assessment*. S. Doc. No. 97–998, 97th Congress, 2nd Session, Feb. 5, 1982.

———. Commission on the Operation of the Senate. *Congressional Support Agencies: A Compilation of Papers*. S. Doc. No. 94–278, 94th Congress, 2nd Session, Dec. 1976.

———. Committee on Foreign Relations. Subcommittee on Arms Control. *Analysis of the Effects of Limited Nuclear War*. Committee Print, 94th Congress, 1st Session, Sep. 1975.

———. Committee on Rules and Administration. Subcommittee on Computer Services. "Technology Assessment for the Congress." Hearing on S.2302 and H.R.10243, 92nd Congress, 2nd Session, Mar. 2, 1972.

———. Committee on Rules and Administration. Subcommittee on Computer Services. *Technology Assessment Act of 1972*. S. Report 92–1123, 92nd Congress, 2nd Session, Sep. 13, (Legislative Day Sep. 12), 1972.

———. Committee on Rules and Administration. Subcommittee on Computer Services. "Technology Assessment for the Congress." Committee Print, 92nd Congress, 2nd Session, Nov. 1, 1972.

Shapley, Deborah. "OTA Funds are Up Against the (West Front) Wall." *Science* 181 (1973), p. 928.

Sharfman, Peter. "On the Uses of OTA Reports." Unpublished document, 1983, OTA Archive AC #243, Washington, D.C.

Shevitz, Jeffrey M. "Some Issues From the History and Operation of the United States Office of Technology Assessment." Paper Prepared for Vienna, Austria, OECD Meeting, Jun. 1989.

Smith, Bruce L.R. *U.S. Science Policy since World War II*. Washington, D.C.: Brookings Institution, 1990.

Smith, James Allen. *Brookings at Seventy-Five*. Washington, D.C.: Brookings Institution, 1991.

Smits, Ruud and Jos Leyten. "Key Issues in the Institutionalization of Technology Assessment." *Futures* 20 (Feb. 1988), pp. 19–36.

Southwick, Thomas P. "Hill Technology Assessment Office Hit by Controversy, Future Role is Questioned." *Congressional Quarterly*, Jun. 18, 1977, pp. 1202–1203.

Stark, Fortney. Statement in *The Congressional Record*. 103rd Congress, 2nd Session, Apr. 1, 1993, p. H1851.

Sundquist, James. *The Decline and Resurgence of Congress*, Washington, D.C.: The Brookings Institution, 1981.

Teague, Olin. Statement in *The Congressional Record*. 92nd Congress, 2nd Session, Feb. 8, 1972, p. 3200.

————. Letter to Emilio Daddario, OTA Director, (with accompanying report), Dec. 22, 1976. OTA Correspondence Files, Washington, D.C.

Thurber, James A. "Policy Analysis on Capitol Hill: Issues Facing the Four Analytic Support Agencies of Congress." *Policy Sciences Journal* 6 (1977), pp. 101–111.

Tower, John. Statement in *The Congressional Record*. 95th Congress, 1st Session, Aug. 4, 1977, pp. 26950–26951.

Udall, Morris and Ted Stevens. Letter to OTA Director John Gibbons, May 5, 1980. OTA Correspondence Files, Washington, D.C.

U.S. Congress. Budget and Accounting Act of 1921. 67th Congress, 1st Session, Jun. 10, 1921.

Vig, Norman. "Parliamentary Technology Assessment in Europe: A Comparative Perspective," in Gary C. Bryner, ed., *Science, Technology, and Politics: Policy Analysis in Congress*. Boulder: Westview, 1922, pp. 209–226.

Wanniski, Jude. "Teddy Kennedy's 'Shadow Government.'" *The Wall Street Journal*, Mar. 27, 1973, p. 20.

Webber, David J. "Political Conditions Motivating Legislators' Use of Policy Information." *Policy Studies Review* 4(1) (Aug. 1979), pp. 110–118.

Weinberg, Alvin. "Topics and Questions in Science Advising," in Kenneth W. Thompson, ed. *The Presidency and Science Advising*, Vol. VII. New York: University Press of America, 1990, pp. 103–114.

Weiss, Carol. "Congressional Committees as Users of Analysis." *Journal of Policy Analysis and Management* 8(3) (1989), pp. 411–431.

Wildavsky, Aaron B. *The New Politics of the Budgetary Process*. Glenview, Ill.: Scott, Foresman and Company, 1988.

Whiteman, David. "The Fate of Policy Analysis in Congressional Decision Making: Three Types of Use in Committees." *Western Political Quarterly* 38(2) (Jun. 1985), pp. 294–311.

Wright, James C., Jr. "The View from Capitol Hill," in William H. Robinson and Clay H. Wellborn, *Knowledge, Power and the Congress*. Washington, D.C.: Congressional Quarterly Press, 1991, pp. 1–4.

Wright, Joseph R. "Testimony on Downsizing the Legislative Branch Support Agencies." Joint House-Senate Legislative Appropriations Subcommittee, U.S. House of Representatives and Senate. Unpublished version, Feb. 2, 1995.

INDEX